To Gil, with my love.

© Joan Simcock

POWER PUBLICATIONS
1 Clayford Avenue
Ferndown
Dorset. BH22 9PQ

ISBN 1 898073 18 X

Original drawings and front cover: Joan Simcock
Layout: Mike Power

This is a true story, and inevitably I have included in it the people who were an important part of our lives at the time.

I am grateful to them all, and in order to spare them any embarrassment, I have given them fictitious names.

Joan Simcock

Chapter 1

"There's no loo" I said feebly. It was the only practical observation I could muster as we stood looking over the low hedge to where broad bands of green, divided by thin hedgerows, stretched before us like a luscious layer cake. In the circumstances it was a carping remark, and quite inaccurate. There was a loo. It was a breeze block sentry box with a wooden door and a corrugated roof, standing at the farthest end of the long, narrow back garden and conveniently situated next to a huge, well matured compost heap which was crazily but firmly held in control by four rusty bedheads, their brass knobs black with age and exposure to the elements, nodding drunkenly at each corner.

At that moment practicalities seemed out of place as the heady scent of honeysuckle enveloped us. Clumps of pale primroses dotted the bank at the far side of the nearest field, where three tall oaks stood abreast, casting their shade on a herd of black and white Friesians huddled gossiping by the gate, jaws ceaselessly rotating and tails rhythmically swishing.

Here and there ash trees grew, and smaller oaks, their delicate green leaves shimmering in the spring sunshine. Against the skyline rose a small spinney of straight elms and birches, whilst to the north the fields rolled gently like a giant tumulus upward and over towards the backdrop of birch and larch, now green, now silver as the wind stirred the leaves. Plump grey wood pigeon rose in scattered flight from the tops of trees, and with a staccato flap of wings vanished from sight into the woods. Nature had brought out all her wares to tempt and delight us, and we were powerless to resist.

Gil took great exaggerated sniffs of warm air. "Sheer Constable" he said, putting an arm round my shoulders and gazing at the landscape so fresh and vigorous with new life, "except that Constable never used such outrageous colours".

"I don't know whether you've noticed" I said, reading the agent's particulars, and forcing myself to look at things objectively, thereby striking another discordant note, "there's no electricity".

Smiling persuasively, Gil dismissed it with "Have you though how romantic oil lamps could be?"

I had not until then, but started to and was carried away for a moment by delicious visions of cosy dinners by candlelight, plying the beloved with my exotic culinary creations, ignoring the probability that if our anxiously calculated resources proved sufficient to buy this place, they were unlikely to run to the luxury of a table at which to tempt him. But as we stood there Old Mother Nature's magical sales talk had cast its spell. We both knew that my objections were merely tokens, and we were certain without saying a word to each other that our search had ended. We knew now without doubt that our future was here, working together and learning to make a living from the soil.

Three years had elapsed since the war which had gobbled us up in our teens, pitched us into the unfamiliar life of the Armed Forces, and spat us out in our twenties, leaving us, the fortunate ones, to our restless adjustment to the peace. Gil was still in the R.A.F. when I met him, having spent his service years flying fighter planes, totally absorbed in the comradeship and excitement

4

of life at a precarious level. The emergency over, however, for him the sense of purpose had receded, and finding himself becoming increasingly impatient with the pomposity and pettiness of the Service in peacetime, decided that his future lay elsewhere.

During those same years I had chosen to make my quite un-noteworthy contribution to Hitler's downfall by joining the ranks of khaki clad women and entering a hitherto unimagined world of parade ground drill, flat lace-up shoes, of censored letters home, and sleeping twenty-two to a Nissen hut. Five years later, clutching a one way Railway Warrant, civilian clothing allowance (unlike the men who were issued with quite awful shiny suits and trilby hats) and with a sense of freedom tinged with apprehension and sadness at the loss of friends made and mislaid all over the country, I went home, like Gil already feeling for the way back and seeking, not only somewhere to put down roots after years of rootlessness, but a whole new and fulfilling way of life.

For six months we had looked at a dreary succession of market gardens and nurseries, with and without accommodation, most comically described as desirable, appealing or quaint, and most within our price range had, on inspection, turned out to be tumbledown shacks which looked as if they would never last the day, and (this being carefully omitted from the agent's particulars) adjacent to a gasworks where the scent of honeysuckle would have come a very poor second, or with an uninterrupted view of the local coal yard or abattoir.

"No thank you," we said, until we began to sound like a badly cracked record, "it isn't exactly what we're looking for." One suave young man remarked, unable to disguise his boredom, "You mean you want something better for less".

"Got it in one," Gil replied "please do what you can".

When the details of "The Homestead" arrived in the post one morning, we were justifiably cynical, but like the drowning man clutching at a straw we were desperate enough to consider anything, and although by this time conditioned to disappointment, we set off to view in a mood of cautious optimism with Tack, our Welsh corgi, on the back seat, his ears pricked with excitement at the chance of a jaunt in the car and, with any luck, a walk. He was a back seat driver with a difference, concerned only with the standard of driving behind us, standing up on his hind legs throughout the journey barking furiously at anyone who was not keeping his distance.

The breathtaking quality of the April afternoon added to our enjoyment as we drove into the Dorset countryside through banks sprinkled with celandine and daisies, and hedges white with hawthorn blossom, through the old Minster town of Wimborne and down a quiet lane where the glint of sun on glasshouses could be seen through a privet hedge. Getting out of the car and walking into the short drive, we peered through the pink budded low branches of an old apple tree and saw a diminutive thatched cottage squatting like a speckled hen in the spring sunshine.

The garden consisted mostly of well kept lawn, with a gravel path running

5

up through the centre to the dark green front door. Daffodils grew abundantly in the flower beds, and in a thick white and gold band around the base of the apple tree, whose trunk had split and become, as it were, three trees joined only by the roots. Down one side of the lawn was a narrow bed of standard roses behind which a thick, gleaming laurel hedge provided seclusion from the lane. On the opposite side three macracarpa trees, squarely clipped, stood at precise intervals like sentinels, and between them clusters of peonies and monkshood. A small stream ran parallel between shallow banks, flanked by the honeysuckle hedge over which we looked into the adjoining field.

Tack was bustling about in a state of euphoria, sniffing at every blade of grass and thrusting an enquiring nose into the laurel, his short excited barks several octaves higher than usual. Wagging his stump of a tail was not enough to express his joy. The whole of his small sturdy brown body was undulating from stem to stern. As a final seal of approval, he crashed through the orderly daffodils and lifted his leg lingeringly and repeatedly against the apple tree. A choice of three trunks simultaneously was undreamed of bliss to a town bred dog, and temptation had triumphed over good manners.

He scampered after us as we went up the path to introduce ourselves to Mrs Burden, the owner occupier, a smiling, middle-aged lady who, without benefit of modern conveniences had lived all her married life in the cottage, had borne and reared her fine brood of three sons and a daughter. Now, duty done and her children grown and some with families of their own, she looked forward with delight to settling in a bright, shining aseptic bungalow with water from a tap and light which appeared at the flick of a switch.

The door of the cottage opened straight into the living room, which in contrast to the brilliant sunshine was so gloomy that it took us several seconds to adjust our eyes to the remarkable scene. A wooden partition had been erected for warmth or privacy, perhaps both, which stretched half the length of the room. The ceiling was covered with asbestos sheets and was so low that Gil stood uncomfortably with bowed head and sagging knees, looking rather like a schoolboy summoned to the Headmaster's study.

In fact there was very little standing room in any direction, such was the clutter of furniture. Several chairs were placed up to an enormous table in the centre, and against the far wall facing the door was an upright piano above which hung large framed photographs of King George V and his Queen gazing imperiously out over the ledge of her bejewelled bosom. Flagstones undulated crazily on the floor, and the walls which were covered with flower patterned paper leaned and bulged.

An aggressive black cooking stove, which I knew disliked me on sight, jutted out into the room, and above it sad dark red material edged with bobbles was nailed along a narrow mantelshelf, and along a cupboard opening under the small window. Dark red curtains hung at the window and covered the lower half of a black wooden cupboard which was cemented into the floor, presumably since it contained china and looked in grave danger of falling over on the uneven floor.

On either side of the stove was a recess, one of which was a bake oven with a small square opening, not unusual in this type of cottage. The other contained a large zinc copper. Beside the copper stood a dome-shaped cage in which perched a large green parrot thoughtfully scratching behind its head and ignoring us. That is until it turned its head and spotted Tack. The scratching abruptly stopped, the claw remained where it was in mid-air, and peering down to dog level it screeched "HELLO!" Tack froze in horror, one front paw raised, and never one to show outstanding courage in the face of the enemy, turned and fled out of the cottage and down the path, his ears pointed backwards and his short Welsh mountain legs scarcely touching the ground.

We went through the second door of the living room into the kitchen which, probably because of the frugality of its furnishings, seemed lighter and larger. This was the only favourable comment I could think of since it was quite unlike any kitchen I had ever seen. The total absence of basic equipment such as a sink and draining board made me realise just what the lack of running water and electricity, until now taken for granted, would mean. My heart went out to Mrs Burden, and I silently saluted her for her fortitude and ingenuity, for ingenious indeed she must have been to care for her family in such circumstances. All the same, it was cheerful with a faint lingering smell of cooking, and the sunlight came through the small casement window, bouncing off the gleaming pots and pans on the wall, and onto the warm flagstones.

We went up the winding staircase which led out of the kitchen into a landing bedroom and through to the one main bedroom which was quite large, with a higher ceiling than the ground floor. The walls were covered with a startling blue and silver paper, like Christmas wrapping, which shone brightly in the light from the small window. A deep narrow recess was made by a huge chimney breast which stretched from floor to ceiling. We were told that this was a cradle nook which must have held many generations of babies like, it seemed to me, an old warm protective nanny, until her charges had grown and gone, and now she sat empty lapped, silently waiting. Only a solitary Painted Lady butterfly was there, wings furled, which had overwintered in the deepest corner and had not yet woken to its ephemeral spring.

We came out once more into the sunshine and down the path past the doorless double garage to a small orchard which Tack had already discovered, and nose to ground was so busy sizing up the possibilities that he barely had time to acknowledge our arrival. Fruit trees, apple, plum and pear, perhaps sixteen in all, were showing their tight pink and white blossom and promised a generous yield. Daffodils grew at random in the long grass by a well, to which we noticed was fitted a semi-rotary pump.

Level with it was a small propogating house, and beyond were three glass-houses filled with neat rows of tomato plants. A blast of warm air met us as we opened the doors and we lingered in the sweet, damp, earthy smell, exclaiming at the sturdiness of the young plants.

Walking back to the car, having taken leave of Mrs Burden, we were reluctant to go, and paused to look round, feeling that this place was ours already. Standing there in the warm April sunshine we experienced a feeling of belonging, a reassuring sense of continuity which the transitory life of the Services had taken from us. As we drove home, we discussed every aspect, knowing in our hearts that the decision had been made but feeling the need to list the facts objectively. We were neither of us accustomed to a rural existence, but considered that an advantage, and relished the thought of distancing ourselves from towns.

We knew nothing at all about growing crops under glass, or any other way for that matter, but we could learn. Having done our sums, we knew that we would have very little to live on, and could expect no profit from the crops, if they survived in our inexpert hands, for a considerable time. We were slightly uneasy about the lack of the most basic amenities, but such was our euphoria that we brushed that aside as a secondary problem. Neither of us was deluded into expecting a soft life but, come hell or high water, it was what we wanted, living by our own efforts and making the cottage into a home.

All angles considered, in complete agreement, excited and already sure of Tack's vote, we drove straight to the astonished estate agent to stake our claim to The Homestead, and immediately set a date for our wedding.

* * * * *

We stood together on the lawn, while Tack joyfully renewed his already considerable acquaintance with the apple tree, whose widespread branches now showed promise of a bumper crop of fruit. Bees were busy gathering their harvest in the deep pink recesses of the flowering currant bush. As we paused to look around us, breathing in the sweet scent of roses, a butterfly alighted for a moment on my arm, and was gone.

We were sure that Tack had enjoyed our honeymoon, swimming with us in the warm waters of Tallands Cove, lying in the shade of the tall rocks, and walking on the cool evening sands when a soft breeze blew in from the gently lapping ocean. We pottered about the small villages with their entrancing patterns of shells embedded in the whitewashed walls of the cottages, browsing in the diminutive front rooms turned gift shops for the season, and sat out at café tables hungrily eating fresh caught lobster, listening to the soft voices of the Cornish people.

There had never been any doubt in our minds that Tack would come with us, but we found that very few hoteliers were enthusiastic about canine guests. One lady, however, expressed herself willing to accommodate him provided that we could guarantee his good behaviour. This we promptly did in glowing terms, assuring her that we should be out a great deal of our time and that he could be relied upon to behave impeccably throughout his stay.

To be fair, through no fault of his, our earnest pledge lost some of its credibility on the morning after our arrival when, late to rise and on our way out of the hotel, he bounded ahead of us down the stairs, pausing only to lift an ecstatic leg against the highly glossed front door post. What seemed like an endless stream flowed down the three stone steps to the garden path and into the serried ranks of lobelia and scarlet salvia, as precise as a brigade of guards.

"Oh, TACK!" I said in horror.

"Oh, God!" said Gil.

Suddenly we were looking into the furious eyes of the Proprietor, a thin faced lady with a switch-on, switch-off smile, who appeared to resent the intrusion of her guests. She hissed that she had, against her better judgement, made a SPECIAL CONCESSION in permitting a dog, and she said the word with distaste, and she hoped that the fouling of her establishment would not occur again.

"Now," she said with the brisk chilly smile of a headmistress, "you've had your scolding. Off you go". Adding as an afterthought, "Have a pleasant day". Apologising, and half expecting to be given a hundred lines for our misdemeanour, we followed the cause of our embarrassment, by this time relieved and anxious to press on to explore the new and exciting smells that Cornwall had to offer, down the path and out of the gate.

Bidding farewell to the lady at the end of what was to be our last holiday for longer than we knew, we noted that she was now amiably disposed towards us, and would not have been surprised to read "Have done well this term after a poor start" as a footnote to our bill.

I reminded Tack of all this as he excitedly darted in every direction like a clockwork toy with defective mechanism. He ignored me, too busy to pay attention as, in the traditional manner, I was carried over the threshold of our new home. Or that was the intention. We had forgotten that the door measured only five feet four inches and Gil considerably more. It was to be some time before we learned to duck our heads on entering, and many a headache resulted.

We stood in the middle of the absurd little room, empty now of all but the wooden cupboard cemented into the flagstones, and the old black stove scowling at us. We flung open the window, and the dark red bobbles along the mantelshelf bespangled walls leaned and twinkled as we hugged each other and began to laugh.

9

Chapter 2

According to a friend who had extensive knowledge of old buildings, our cottage was aged between two hundred and fifty and three hundred years. We were awestruck by this fact, and very impressed with the surveyor's report, which suggested that it had weathered its time well. It had been a cattle drover's dwelling, typical of many found in Dorset, built by the man himself slowly and laboriously on a small patch of land given to him by his employer, a farmer or landowner. In return he tended the cattle, receiving a minimal wage and such perquisites as a milk cow and free firewood, growing his own vegetables to keep his often large family fed.

A certain clay content in the earth was needed to build the cottage, and was dug from the nearest source and brought to the site by horse and cart. Water from the stream was then added, and the mixture bound with bracken, gorse, pine needles and heather, sprigs of which we found intact and still colourful when we had reason to knock a hole in the wall. It is said that where you see two or three such cottages close together, not far away you will find a dell resulting from the excavations of those homesteaders hundreds of years ago. One such dell exists near our cottage. It belongs to friends, and is an extension of their large garden, and is beautiful in spring with a carpet of daffodils, primroses and bluebells.

The walls were pebble dashed, giving it its speckled appearance, and sloping steeply down and overhanging the small casement windows was layer upon layer of Dorset straw pinned securely in place by spars, lengths of split hazel cut from the hedgerow and twisted and doubled over in a hairpin shape.

On the west side facing the lane, adjoining the living room was a high bare barnlike room in which the drover had housed his cow in deep winter. It had a separate door, and was in its original state, with an earth floor. Rafters and thatch were exposed, and elderly long vacated cobwebs hung in thick grey festoons, almost to head height. This would one day make a large and attractive room, but in the meantime it was valuable storage space for items of furniture, packing cases, suitcases, bicycles, and indeed anything which was for the moment surplus to requirement.

To our dismay, we were soon aware of the presence of rats there. We seldom saw one, but on opening the door the rustling and scurrying was evidence enough. "Well" we said, "that can be Tack's department". We soon discovered, however, that ratting was not one of Tack's accomplishments. We tried urging him in, hissing "RATS" in excited voices to give him encouragement, but he blundered about making so much noise and commotion that only a half witted, stone deaf rat would have come within yards.

"We'll have to get a cat" said Gil, at which Tack drew back his lip in a curl of contempt and snarled.

"You shouldn't have said that. You've offended him." And to prove me right he stalked off to roll on the compost heap, a habit he had when he particularly wanted to annoy. The compost heap was far superior in odour and consistency to anything he had ever known as a town dog, when at best all he could hope to come across when out for a walk was a decomposed crow. There were definite advantages to living in the country, and it was plain he was going to make the most of every one of them.

He did have some problems though. There were sixteen of them in a coop in the orchard. An assortment of old brown hens which we had taken over with the property. Since they were all O.A.P.s of the poultry world, they were barely a paying proposition , as the number of eggs they laid between them failed to meet the cost of their food, and we could not afford passengers. But they were doing their best, and it was a surprise and delight to open the door at the back of the coop and find one of two eggs, brown and warm, in the straw. "Good girls" we said, "keep it up".

We let them out during the day to scratch about in the orchard, and it infuriated Tack to turn around when he was on one of his nature studies to find them moving stealthily up on him. He had never before seen a hen, and clearly could not quite place them in his category of creatures. They certainly could not claim kinship with the noble dog, and by Heaven, he knew a cat when he saw one! Their strange noises unnerved him, and it was quite obvious that they had nothing to do, like chasing the postman or burying a bone and having to remember where, sometimes months hence. So having decided that their activities were trivial and without point, he set about livening them up a little by chasing them round the orchard, and the resulting stampede, accompanied by flying feathers, clucking and outraged squawks, resembled the unlikely spectacle of elderly ladies in a pillow fight, and brought us running to the scene, trying not to laugh , to administer a severe scolding.

In a very short time, the Wellsomers especially, succumbed to old age, and simply died with no visible sign of disease. We buried them deep behind the propogating house away from Tack's enquiring nose. Most of the survivors, Light Sussex and the stronger breed, found their way to our table. Neither of us could carry out the executions, calling on the good services of a neighbour to whom it was no more than swatting a fly, and although they were a welcome addition to our simple diet, it was not easy to eat one's friends, and we carefully avoided remarks like "Are we having Doris tonight?" We drew the line at Pok Pok, as we called her because it best described the odd little noise she made. She had made up her mind that she would not suffer the fate of her sisters, and attached herself to us, running up the garden to us when we called, head down, feet splayed and wings flapping. When we stroked her shiny back she crouched low, stamping her feet in ecstasy. Tack was quite happy to tolerate one of the silly creatures, and they shared the garden companionably.

It was not long before she decided she would like to accompany us when we strolled up the lane in the fading light of the evening, as a Senior Citizen of the birds feeling it her privilege to dictate her own bedtime, and looking so comical strutting daintily behind us that she never failed to make us laugh.

Leisurely strolls were a rare pleasure for us, those first weeks being a succession of long, hot exhausting days. We literally camped in the cottage while we gave all our attention to our means of livelihood. The crop was by now touching the roofs of the houses, the stems thick and sturdy and bearing trusses of well formed fruit, almost all of which was of the highest quality, leaving us in no doubt of our predecessors' knowledge of their trade. Aware of our ignorance, and perhaps a little sad to leave to our tender mercies the crop they had so carefully nurtured from seedlings, they had left us helpful snippets of information on names and dates, and relevant comments on each, which they had scribbled or pinned on the inside of the doors, with a reminder not to paint the doors or the precious notes would be eliminated.

We pored over books with such intriguing titles as "Tomatoes for Beginners", "How to grow Tomatoes for Profit" and "Half-crowns from Heaven", and shrank from the possibility that our beautiful crop might be overtaken and destroyed by pests and diseases with such blood curdling names as BOTRYTIS,

RED SPIDER and even more sinister, BLOSSOM END ROT, and kept constant vigil for the dreaded symptoms.

We learned to grade them meticulously according to size, shape and quality and packed them in skips covered by white, pink and white, and blue paper which denoted their category. We sat out in the hot sun, brown as two chestnuts, packing, weighing, admiring, discarding, loving the smell and the feel of the smooth shining skins, handling them with care in order that no calyx should be dislodged.

We continued with the retail round established by the Burdens, our customers consisting of householders within a small radius, and two local greengrocers. Three times a week we loaded the van with our precious cargo, paper bags and a set of scales, and Gil set off to call on the "regulars" and drum up fresh trade, while I stayed behind in case of casual customers who, as we were a mile from the main road, were few and far between. Our least favourite among them was Miss Mountford, a school mistress who drove up to the gate in her small car, sounding her horn imperiously until one of us appeared to take her order. She remained in the car while we picked for her, snatched them briskly from us and drove away leaving us open mouthed and empty handed. When, after several visits, we were impertinent enough to remind her of the sum owing, she flushed with annoyance, saying "Well, really!" and almost flung the money down before continuing up the lane.

We knew that twice a week we could expect Amaryllis Foster, a plump middle-aged lady who wore her pince-nez at a jaunty angle, and arrived on her motorised bicycle, her full cotton skirt tucked between her sturdy thighs to prevent it from catching in the spokes of the wheels. She always asked for chats, the very small tomatoes the size of a marble, which were sweet, cheap and difficult to locate. One of us ploughed through each lane of trusses, followed at a brisk trot by Miss Foster, talking incessantly like a rapid firing machine gun, and trilling with laughter as she recounted to us snippets of local gossip about people we had not yet met, and earnest and vivid accounts of how she had danced naked in the dew at dawn. She did not say why, obviously assuming we knew, and we never liked to ask thinking it might be an old Dorset custom and not wanting to admit our ignorance.

As a divertissement we were treated to regular revolting details of the ailments sent to try her Manchester terrier, which sometimes came with her, sitting up front in the bicycle basket with a tuft of hair on the top of his head tied up with red ribbon, cross about it and yapping to be free to sink his tiny teeth into something or someone.

She darted about the glasshouse in her leather sandals, pouncing on a chat here and a chat there, and with a cry of victory downing it with a gulp. The paper bag filled up slowly. Miss Foster filled up far quicker, so that she took away two pounds for the price of one. By the time she remounted and took off up the lane, buzzing at full throttle like an angry bee, we were left limp, laughing and out of pocket.

One of my daily chores was learning to control the hosepipe, since the plants needed more liquid refreshment than a Works Outing. It responded docilely to

Gil's handling, recognising the master, but it reserved its nastiest habits for me, like suddenly twisting itself, and with a roar and a snarl, ejecting a breathtaking douche of cold water into my face, or spitefully snaking its nozzle into my shoe until it squelched. I always ended up wetter than the plants, and the job done, staggered out of the humid atmosphere scarlet faced and wilting like a wax effigy on bonfire night.

The water for this operation, for which we paid twenty-five shillings a year, was piped across the road from a nursery which covered an area of twenty acres. A vast sea of glass from which were picked, packed and marketed each week tons of tomatoes, and many other crops besides. The arrangement worked well most of the time, but if there was particularly heavy watering over there all that came our way was a miserable trickle, and it took us a whole frustrating morning to water one house.

All domestic water came from the well down in the orchard, the semi-rotary pump driving the water out of a tap into buckets. Taking the empty buckets down the hundred foot path was one thing. Bringing them back full was quite another. They started full, but with each step a little water slopped over the sides, so that by the time we reached the kitchen the buckets were only half full and the path awash.

After daily practice we developed a kind of gliding gait with knees slightly bent and arms straight to the side, which when perfected, if it did little for our posture, helped to keep the water in and saved us several journeys a day. Gil said helpfully "Look on the bright side. If we do this long enough we'll be able to tie our shoelaces without stooping".

Washing and rinsing clothes was done at the well as our only means of heating water was in kettles on our two primus stoves. Sometimes I looked at the cloudless blue sky and longed for a pouring wet day so that I could just peg everything out on the line and allow nature to do my rinsing for me.

It was our personal ablutions which presented the greatest problem. Standing in a small bowl on the flagstones in the kitchen sponging ourselves down was tolerable on those summer days, but thoroughness was limited and movement restricted in order to retain water in the bowl. My longing for a bath began to border on the neurotic, and I started poring over magazine pictures of luxury bathrooms the size of the cottage, in which shapely, smiling, nude and semi-nude ladies languished up to their scented armpits in steaming foam. Sitting in my sweaty shirt and tomato stained trousers and feeling like a polecat, I hated them. Having no friends near enough to be called upon to lend us their baths, we decided we would have to get to know our immediate neighbours, and in time were fortunate and very grateful to the foreman of the large nursery and his wife, who gave us weekly use of their bathroom, with a generous glass of sherry after our ablutions to set the seal on the occasion.

In the meantime, to our delight, we found hanging on a wall in the store room a large zinc bath, in which we could sit with our knees tucked up under our chins. Nothing looked more beautiful. That was unbelievable luxury! The water was heated in the kettles, and there was never more than just enough to sit in, but it was pure joy. The ceremony of the FIRST BATH took a rather

frivolous turn when we decided to open the remaining bottle of wedding champagne which we were keeping for some special occasion. Nothing could be more special than this, and the hilarity grew as we toasted each other from tea mugs, and emptied the steaming kettles over half a pound of sweet smelling bath salts.

On the principle of "ladies first", I had first dip, then Gil poured away the water into the stream, staggering under the weight, and more kettles were boiled for him. Tack entered into the spirit of it, and after a tot or two began excitedly circling the bath, licking off the soap as fast as we could lather ourselves. Draining my mug and scrubbing Gil's back, I said "I wonder if a magazine would be interested in OUR luxury bathroom."

"More likely, the way this is going, to be interested in an article about orgies."

"The dictionary definition of an orgy is a riotous, licentious or drunken revel."

"Quite. Better make sure the curtains are properly drawn. The neighbours may not be ready for this sort of thing and we might be drummed out of Dorset."

Tack meanwhile, exhausted from his alcoholic capers, and afraid it could be his turn for a bath, had staggered to his basket and was curled up fast asleep and snoring loudly. We decided to follow his example, and I began to mop up the floor and tidy away the paraphernalia of washing, while Gil put on his dressing gown and went down for a last look at the glasshouses, pausing to say goodnight to Pok Pok on the way. For some time she had foresaken the coop at night, and for reasons we could not fathom, had put herself to bed high up in the pear tree, fiercely resisting any attempt to bring her down. We were afraid for her safety because of the foxes which came into the garden, but she was so vehemently opposed to the coop that we pandered to an old lady's whim and left her there. She came to no harm in her tree, and Gil shone his torch on her on his way down to reassure himself. There she was, curled up like a fat feather ball in the fork of the tree, and there she stayed until morning light when we heard her tap, tap on the door reminding us that it was her breakfast time.

"All's well", said Gil, returning to the cottage, "and the nightingale's singing again".

We stood at the door, listening to our nightly serenade from somewhere in the second field, and thinking ourselves very fortunate indeed to have been singled out for such delight. The pure notes soared into the night sky, filling the stillness of the countryside with their beauty, and the poignancy of those moments remains with us still.

We said goodnight to Tack, who was now banished to the living room. At first he had slept in the bedroom with us, but his habit of leaving his basket several times a night in order to scratch himself and thumping on the bare boards drove us to a frenzy.

Blowing out the lamp, we lit two candles and took them up the creaking, winding staircase, climbing thankfully into bed. Occasionally we were subjected to what we called, among other names less printable, our PROMS NIGHT, and as soon as we settled down we knew that this was to be one of them. A family of starlings had moved in under the unwired thatch, and held regular jamborees, twittering and scritch-scratching until in fury we banged on the ceiling. This shocked them into temporary silence and started Tack barking.

Sometimes the rats in the store room took up the refrain playing tag and gnawing steadily at the woodwork. I am sure we slept eventually, but what seemed to us five minutes later the dawn chorus, rendered with boisterous exultation by the massed birds of the entire Southern Counties, dragged us unwillingly back to consciousness, and as a grand finale was backed by the early morning goods train which whistled and chuffed its cheery way through the countryside. We cursed it, and pulling the pillows down over our heads, fall into a deep sleep until the alarm clock shrilled its tyrannical reminder of another day.

Chapter 3

No matter how disturbed his night, Gil is what is known as a cheerful riser, a characteristic I had failed to look into before marriage, and which came as quite a shock. Though greatly improved with the years, I was then incapable of coherent, let alone scintillating conversation very early in the morning, whereas Gil whistled and sang as he shaved, sloshing about merrily and noisily in his washing water.

"It's grounds for divorce, your disgusting cheerfulness," I grumbled one day, trying to focus on my cornflakes. "Metabolic imcompatability."

"Big words for this time of the morning. That's no grounds for divorce. Marriage to a zombie could be though, " he added thoughtfully.

I grinned and glanced at the shelf where, among the pots and pans, sat a small china donkey, cream in colour, with enormous ears. The eyes were mournful and the bags underneath gave it a comically liverish expression.

"I had to buy it," Gil had said, bringing it home a few days before. "It so reminded me of you in the morning."

Tack always joined us for breakfast, having eaten his rather quickly and always hopeful of an extra in the way of bacon rind or fried bread, and it was not long before we heard the familiar tap, tap on the front door announcing Pok Pok's descent from the pear tree, and reminding us that there was another mouth, or rather beak, to feed. When we opened the door she minced primly into the kitchen, greeting us with low, sweet crooning, and waiting patiently for her meal, washing it down with a long drink from Tack's water bowl.

Gil returned to the glasshouses, having already put in an hour's work before breakfast, leaving me to do the minimal chores required to keep the cottage habitable. I stood on the doorstep watching him go in the fresh fragrance of the early day. The blackbird gave us his usual greeting from high in the apple tree, his joyful song ringing out over the garden, still misty with the promise of another warm day.

Washing up was a simple matter, using two bowls on a small table, one for washing and one for rinsing, ladling the water out of a bucket with a small saucepan, and adding a kettleful of boiling water. We thought we were rather well organised with our two primus stoves, and two Valor oil stoves on another table, one of which was fitted with a small tin oven. A tremendous find this, brought in his van to our door by the paraffin man, who called me Mrs Oomps and made weekly visits, Tuesday being his day for delivery. The sound of the cheerful horn was accompanied by the rattling, clanking and tinkling of pots, pans, tin bowls and a hundred different utensils which hung and swayed on hooks inside. It was Aladdin's cave, smelling of paraffin, methylated spirits, lavender furniture polish and candles, and I always looked forward to his arrival, eagerly jumping aboard to see what treasures there were to be bought, while he drank a mug of tea and brought us up to date with the local social activities. He enjoyed calling on us, saying obligingly on one occasion, "If you want me very badly, Mrs Oomps, I can come again on Thursday".

Our appetites were enormous, fanned by the combination of physical exertion and good Dorset air, and we ate our way through ten large loaves a week, I have to admit, from the local bakery, new and crusty and far more delicious than any loaf I could have produced in my primitive little oven, and delivered to the door three times a week in hail, rain or shine and sometimes as late as nine o'clock at night by a cheerful fellow called Mac. Eaten with our cheese rations for agricultural workers – I think ten ounces per person per week – and shallots pulled from the back garden, they were scrumptious and filling.

I was no Fanny Craddock, as Gil will confirm, and I suspect that even the redoubtable Fanny would have quailed at the prospect of exchanging her gleaming aseptic kitchen for mine. But after a period of trial and error and some infuriating failures, I managed basic menus including joints of meat when the budget permitted, and graduated to large fruit cakes which quite often turned out well, with no appreciable sag in the middle, depending on what draught found its way into the kitchen.

Added to our diets were the tomatoes that were too mis-shapen to sell, and now as an additional bounty, the fruit trees were fulfilling their promise of a generous yield. We spent hours up ladders, filling baskets and boxes with damsons, greengages, and large Victoria plums, many of which never reached their destination, their delicious juice trickling down our chins. The wasps, sated and tipsy with the heady beverage begrudged us our share and did their best to discourage us, buzzing angrily at our flapping hands.

One of the first apple trees to ripen was an Allington Pippin, in taste and appearance a beautiful fruit, its skin dark red and shiny as satin. There were several other varieties including Non Pareil, Blenheim Orange and Bramley cookers as large as grapefruit which when baked in the oven with brown sugar emerged as soft and fluffy as candy floss and beyond compare.

The fallers, or those which were bruised or in any way imperfect, we put into boxes stacked in the garage for our own use. The "cream" of the harvest were weighed and carefully packed and sold to our retailer who, despite a glut locally, always gave us a good price because he said he could trust us not to hide any 'bad 'uns' at the bottom. Some I took up to the cottage, filling bowls with plums and stacking the remainder under the kitchen table, a new acquisition together with a kitchen cabinet for groceries.

Other than the fruit, perishable food was kept in a small tin safe which hung on a nail on the north wall of the cottage where it was well shaded from the sun by the overhanging thatch. This was not always satisfactory, as the safe had a tendency to blow away in a high wind, and on discovering its absence I spent the next ten minutes chasing the contents downstream, or grovelling in the field in the hope of beating the cows to it. Sometimes, too late, I stood helplessly by watching our week's bacon ration, paper and all, disappearing down a bovine gullet.

Having equipped the kitchen so that it was at least workable, there was a far greater problem to be tackled. We had to rid ourselves of what we called our ARMY OF OCCUPATION, black beetles and mice in large numbers that scuttled and squeaked and took off in all directions when we entered. For the sake of health and hygiene something had to be done, and fast. Sprinkling insecticide on the flagstones each night after Tack was in bed soon discouraged the beetles, but the mice were more persistent and continued to bring their friends. One forsook the kitchen for the living room, setting up house in a hole beneath the window seat. Most evenings, as we sat quietly listening to the wireless, his pale brown head would emerge, large dark eyes glistening in the lamplight and whiskers twitching. He sat motionless for hours, obviously a music lover, until either the programme ended or one of us made an involuntary movement and startled him back into the safety of home. We quite liked his company, but I was unprepared for the liberty taken by one of his family. Reaching up to the shelf in the dark kitchen one evening, it shot out from behind a biscuit tin and dived straight down the neck of my shirt. It is hard to say which of us was the most surprised, and clearly such an error of judgement could not be allowed to become a habit, so we had to take the course which we had been reluctant even to discuss.

As I have already mentioned, Tack was no ratter. He was no better at mousing, and although there was always tremendous excitement, barking and tail wagging and trying to be in six places at once, there was no strategy, no subtlety and seldom a kill.

Gil bought a trap and set it, baiting it with cheese, and we left it on the floor under the window before going to bed. We had scarcely settled our heads on the pillows when there was a loud crack from downstairs. We knew the trap had claimed its inquisitive little victim, and we lay there stiff and miserable, holding hands to comfort one another, and feeling like murderers. Gil sadly removed the small corpse the next morning, and our remorse reminded us of a lady, so the story goes, who, faced with the same problem, put a special gluelike substance down on her window sill, and on coming down in the morning was horrified to find several struggling mice stuck fast. The next recommended step was to administer the coup de grace, but she was so overcome at the prospect that she gently picked off each frantic little creature, wiping its paws clean before setting it free.

She was a woman after my own heart. I have always felt an affection for mice since childhood, when I persuaded my parents, already sharing their home with three children, an overworked and underpaid house parlour maid called Bridget, a dog, two cats, an aviary of tropical birds and a rabbit, into buying me a pair of albinos, which I named Ebb and Flo, and loved dearly. I was allowed to keep them in my bedroom, so that I could watch their antics from my bed, and listen to the comforting sound of their exercise wheel, the conditions laid down, not unreasonably, were that I should keep then scrupulously clean and not allow them to wander about the house unsupervised. Or supervised for that matter, since unbelievably not everyone shared my passion

20

for mice. Things did not go too well, as I failed to keep my side of the bargain. On a mischievous impulse, I ill advisedly put Flo on the back of Bridget's neck, unable to imagine anyone not regarding this as the greatest accolade. Unfortunately, she did not share my view, and screaming "Jesus, Mary and Joseph!" which surely must have been heard across the water in her native Ireland, "Get it off me!" her stricken face as white as her apron, threatened to leave if my mother could not keep the mice and her children, while she was about it, under better control.

Things went from bad to worse after that, as I became bored with the necessity to clean their cage, with the result that the atmosphere in my bedroom became, to say the least, unsavoury. Ebb and Flo were snatched from my heaving bosom and given to a small patient of my father's as an aid to her convalescence. For a few days I mourned, wishing the recipient of my mice anything but a speedy recovery. Then I turned my attention to collecting snails.

But that is by the way, and as our be-whiskered house guests continued to call, we discussed, making certain that Tack was out of earshot, the necessity of keeping a cat.

Chapter 4

August, relentlessly hot still, reduced the lawn to a large loofah, brown and scrubby from the lack of rain. The water in the well was low, and the tall fern in the spinney had already begun to lose its summer brilliance. The stream had dwindled to a tired gurgle, and Tack lay panting under the apple tree, too lethargic to put up more than a token barrage of barking at the neighbouring cat which strolled with deliberate insolence past the gate.

Melting in the humid furnace of the glasshouse, we noted that Pok Pok in her wisdom had gone to ground in the cool depths of the long grass in the orchard, sleeping away her days and emerging at sundown for her evening dust bath on the pathway by the well.

Miss Foster took to arriving wearing a white cotton bonnet, tied under the chin, her statuesque proportions magnificently mobile underneath a loose cotton shift. Much affected by the heat, and greatly to our relief since it meant that for once we would make a profit on the transaction, she chose not to help us pick and sat outside on an upturned bucket, languidly fanning herself with a folded paper bag, her pince-nez, suspended from a black cord, quivering on her bosom like a captive butterfly.

The only one who appeared to be quite unaffected by the weather was Mr Potts, our nearest neighbour, whose Davy Crockett hat, complete with racoon tail, still sat at a jaunty angle on his head. We never saw him without it, winter or summer, and considered the possibility that it was growing out of his scalp.

He and Mrs Potts lived in a small bungalow called "Halcyon" which backed onto the nursery. They led a reclusive life, surrounded by laurel hedges, and our acquaintance never progressed beyond the "Good morning" and Good evening" stage. Mrs Potts was a small birdlike woman who, from what we heard while working in the glasshouse, was grumbled at continually by her husband with never so much as a cheep of defiance, and it seemed to us, listening to the daily monologue, that their home was sadly mis-named and that the poor lady's halcyon days, if indeed she had ever known any, were long past.

Realising the urgency of starting on our domestic improvements in good weather, every moment we could spare from keeping the crop cool and watered, picked and packed, was spent making the living room habitable. We gave it top priority, deciding that we could tackle the bedroom as time permitted. The only concession we made was to cover the startling blue and silver wallpaper with a pale pink distemper wash as a temporary balm to our eyes.

Every morning we trundled the furniture into the garden to give us the maximum working space, taking our meals on the lawn, sitting in armchairs to drink our morning tea, exclusive members of the "Alfresco Club". The possibility of acquiring a reputation for eccentricity did occur to us, but as we were foreigners, that is to say not Dorset born and bred, and so newly arrived, we could expect little else.

We started stripping off the wallpaper, which proved to be a more lengthy process than we had anticipated, as underneath the top layer was another. And another and another, until we came to our sixth layer, each one different in pattern and vying with its predecessor in colourful originality, and owing to the undulation of the walls, creating small pockets harbouring silver fish which slithered out into the daylight to die instantly in the deadly spray of my feverishly aimed Flit gun.

Then came trouble. We found that in many places the paper was the walls' only means of support, and alarmingly large chunks fell away as we gently prised and peeled, exposing areas of yellow cob. Gil mopped his brow saying "These people were no fools. They knew what they were doing when they put one layer on top of another", adding grimly, "it looks as if we're going to have to plaster the whole blasted room".

Our do-it-yourself experience had not yet covered renovating old crumbling cottage walls, and neither of us had visualised tackling anything as advanced at such an early stage, but Gil was wise enough to know that before any plastering could be done, the walls must be filled and cement rendered. Sand we already had in abundance, in small ragged heaps dotted about the nursery, and our only requirement was cement. With our living room, and for all we knew, our cottage, on the verge of collapse, swift action was called for lest the walls, so rudely disturbed from years of slumber beneath their many coloured coverings, should resent it and fall down about our ears like a pack of cards.

"Won't be long", said Gil, trying to look cheerful as he leapt into the van.

"Don't worry", I said airily, convinced that the muscles I had developed in the past few months would not look our of place on Mr Universe, "I'll just prop it up till you get back".

Small though the room was there seemed a vast area of wall to cover. As it was Gil's first encounter with a trowel, the air was rent with curses and howls of frustration as a carefully placed lump slid miserably down the wall. This, I knew, was no reflection on his ability, but due to the extreme absorbency of the walls, which, deserving full marks for improvisation, he moistened with a crop sprayer. This, when filled by a hand pump from a bucket of water, gave out a fine spray and provided the necessary adhesive for the cement.

My role as plasterer's mate was to make endless cups of tea, pump, top up the bucket, pump, murmur words of encouragement and keep Tack, constantly bustling in and out to find out what had happened to his usual walk, from under his feet. Working like a demented beaver, and pausing only for a night's rest and occasional sustenance, he completed the task in two days. As I stood back admiringly, the smell of dampness pervading the cottage, he staggered exhausted but triumphant, out into the garden where he collapsed into an armchair and fell fast asleep.

Once dried out, the result of the rendering was so pleasing that instead of plastering over it as planned, we left the walls in their rough state, covering them with a white distemper wash which to our knowledge remains still.

From our first week in the cottage there had been a number of friends and relatives to see us, curious to know what we had let ourselves in for, and whose reactions varied from envy to pitying disbelief. Much as we enjoyed seeing them and appreciated their visits, we were desperately conscious of the need to use every available hour of daylight in which to make the cottage comfortable before the onset of winter, and felt we were in danger of becoming anti-social and begrudging of time spent with them. But most were understanding and volunteered for some helpful task, and at our invitation picked fruit for themselves, the orchard resounding with laughter and shouts from the tops of ladders. Tomatoes had to be paid for strictly at the going rate, and those we picked for them, fearful for the precious plants in careless hands.

Freddie, our six feet four friend, having learned a painful lesson in the living room, had taken to arriving on hands and knees. Sitting on an orange box, which was the only furniture not out in the garden, he would jump up saying "Well, must be going", and cracking his head on the ceiling as he spoke. Apologetically helping the poor dazed man to his car became a frequent necessity, and if we were not to lose our tall friends and be forced to take up with pygmies, something would have to be done.

Our next major task, therefore, while the walls were drying out, was to remove the asbestos sheets which covered the ceiling, which was well under six feet at the highest end. As Gil started to unscrew the first of the huge sheets, I dashed upstairs to wrap my head in a scarf to prevent any lurking horrors from dropping into my hair. There were many insect visitors of one sort or another in the cottage, and thatch seems to harbour particularly large varieties of spider, some examples of which appeared out of deep, dark corners, reducing me to a state of jibbering idiocy.

"They're much more frightened of you than you are of them" said Gil in the same reasonable, maddening tone my mother had used when I was a child.

"Impossible."

Ashen faced, I averted my eyes as he picked one up and threw it out of the window. I have always fervently believed in the right of my fellow creatures, however small and humble, to life. But irrational fear suggested to me that the only good spider was a dead one. "Not so," said Gil, who loves them like brothers, "they are the gardeners' friends, and should be allowed to thrive".

"Alright. If they're designed to rid our soil of undesirable aliens, why don't they stay out there and get on with it instead of gate-crashing the cottage and scaring the wits out of me?"

Only the day before I was coming through the front door with a joint of beef from the outside safe when one of them, either losing its footing or spotting what it believed to be its prey, dropped with a "PLOP!" onto the meat, crouching there, each black hairy leg an obscenity. I screamed, dropping the plate, meat and spider, the plate shattering into a dozen pieces on the concrete step. The joint, after a shaky wash and brush up, was edible. The spider scuttled off into the safety of the rambler rose and vanished. I believe I was the only one to suffer any lasting damage.

This craven account is simply to explain my agonised anticipation as the last screw came away and we gently lowered the sheet. A gruesome litter of corpses slid off onto the flagstones – wood lice, silver fish, spiders great and small, flies and moths all long dead – but for once my squeamishness took second place to my interest in the ceiling. We saw narrow knotted pine beams, about a foot apart, stretching from front to back of the room, which were in their natural state, with in some places their bark still attached. Now we knew what lay beneath we enthusiastically unfastened the next sheet, and it was not long before all the beams were exposed. We brushed off the cobwebs and the dust of years and suddenly the room seemed lighter, larger and was certainly higher by several inches.

We were pleased with the results of our labours, and while we drank tea and smoked a cigarette we discussed our next task. We disliked the look of the hideous black stove, and I knew without trying that any attempt to cook on it would be met with the same contempt reserved for me by the hosepipe, and we felt that to sit by it in the evenings would be a test of endurance.

So out it had to come. Tea break over, we started to heave and pull, grunting with the exertion, and finally dislodged it and edged it out into the centre of the room. Behind it was a sheet of corrugated tin, which was easily removed. To our utter dismay, there behind that was another, similar stove.

"TWO of the brutes!" I screeched, not believing my eyes.

"It's the same old story. When anything needed renewing, they just covered it with something else."

This discovery stopped us in our tracks, and enthusiasm waning, we suddenly realised how tired and grimy we were, and decided to call it a day. By now the late sun cast long shadows across the garden, splashing the glasshouses

25

with orange and red reflections from its dying rays, and Tack was reminding us that we were not the only hungry ones.

We left stove number two exposed in all its rust and cobwebs and full of ash from its last lighting, and pushed and pulled number one out into the garden where we left it on the path, wishing that some kind fairy would appear while we slept and spirit it away to wherever it is that old stoves go when they have outlived their usefulness. Then we brought in the furniture, piling it higgledy-piggledy in the centre of the room.

We sat nodding over our supper, longing for a hot bath to relax our aching muscles but lacking the energy to go through the rigmarole of bath night. While I washed up, Gil went down to the glasshouses to assure himself that our neglectful day had done the crop no harm, and that Pok Pok was safely on her perch. We staggered up the stairs, defying the starlings and rats to do their worst. Gil was, as usual, first into bed and simultaneously it seemed, he was fast asleep. I was sitting at the dressing table determined, whatever the circumstances, to preserve the ritual of creaming my face, and thinking that in the flickering candlelight it already resembled an elderly prune, when, out of the corner of my eye I saw a movement on the floor by my bare foot and knew instantly that this was going to be a fitting end to a day that would have been an entomologist's delight. As the eight legged monster scuttled past into the farthest corner by the window, with a shriek and a leap which would have done justice to an Olympic gold medallist, I landed on the bed, clutching my nightdress around me and giving no thought to the fact that Gil was until that moment sleeping like the dead.

I have the good fortune to be married to a kindly and patient man, and there are very few situations that send him into a state of uncontrollable fury. One of them, I discovered, is to be woken violently out of a deep sleep, to race round the room in a dim light and grovel under furniture after something which does not wish to be caught, and which merges into the shadows so that it cannot be seen. He leapt out of bed snarling, whilst I cowered, the capture made and the unwelcome visitor snatched up and thrown savagely out of the window, climbed back in muttering dire threats of psychoanalysis.

I maintain that he never really woke throughout the entire operation, and his ability to bound out of bed while still asleep was very impressive. I attributed this hitherto undemonstrated gift to his wartime experiences as a night fighter pilot, and felt sure that had I shouted "SCRAMBLE!" in his ear he would have taken off straight through the roof and into the purple, star scattered sky.

Chapter 5

I was woken, like the sleeping beauty in the fairy tale, with a kiss. Certainly, from what seemed a hundred light years away, I heard the voice of my Prince Charming say "Wake up, slug. Show a leg, Tea's getting cold".

Ungratefully, without opening my eyes, I mumbled, "Go away. It's the middle of the night".

"The sun's shining, the birds have been up for hours, and I've been in the glasshouses since six," he replied cheerfully, "I've done the watering so that we can make an early start."

Consumed with guilt, I sat up and drank the welcome tea, and clambering out of bed, hurried downstairs to wash and start the breakfast. As I glanced through the living room door, stove number two looked balefully at me as if it knew it was about to be trundled out into the garden to join number one. Tack was sitting hungrily and reproachfully in the kitchen, and no dog knew better how to arrange a reproachful look on his face when the occasion demanded. Pok Pok had wandered off, her morning schedule delayed, and had to be recalled with a tattoo beaten on her dish with a spoon.

Tucking into his bacon and tomatoes, Gil said "We'll pick later, shall we? Then we can get a bit done up here first. Let's have a go at the mantelshelf. I've got a feeling we might have a pleasant surprise." First there was mail to be read while we ate. The post arrived at about five thirty each morning, and again later in the day, hail, rain or shine. Our postman sang and whistled as he cycled up the lane and swung into the drive, and if we were about there was a cup of tea for him and some merry banter and cricket talk. There goes a man who is happy with his lot, you would have said. It was with total disbelief, therefore, that we received the news one morning that he had blown away his brains with a shot gun. No explanatory note was left, no reason found at the inquest, and the despair which must have lain behind the cheerful countenance he presented to us all remained a mystery.

This morning, one letter gave us particular pleasure. It was from my cousin Maurice, who came frequently to spend weekends with us, sleeping on a camp bed on the landing. Without exception the starlings and rats did their best to guarantee him a sleepless night, but to no avail. He always declared that nothing ever disturbed him, and the inconvenience of our living conditions bothered him not at all.

He had taken a job in Dorchester, leaving behind his wife in London and living in lodgings until he could find them a permanent home. He was a quiet, deep thinking, gentle man who loved and envied us the peace of the countryside, and looked forward to leaving the town behind him and joining us for a brief respite as much as we enjoyed his company. He could turn his hand to anything and, as he put it, liked to work for his bread and beer. We would look over the gate on Friday evenings and were delighted to see him striding up the lane in his baggy corduroy trousers, knapsack on his back, grinning and waving his pipe at us as he neared the cottage. "You don't live here!" we can remember him saying on his first visit, sheer joy spreading over his face as he stood and looked about him.

He and Gil had not met before our marriage, and instantly liked one another, working well together and talking long and earnestly into the night, sometimes well after my eyes would no longer stay open and I took myself off to bed.

All members of the household fed and watered, we started chipping away the plaster holding the mantelshelf, which turned out to be made not of wood as we had supposed, but of asbestos edged with a wooden strip, and held firmly in place by huge steel pegs. I supported one end while Gil worked on the other, and suddenly the whole shelf, red bobbles and all, came away in a cloud of dust. We were sent reeling by a stench too horrible to describe. Rotting bodies seemed the most likely possibility, and the only explanation could be that some luckless person had been walled up two hundred years ago. We noticed with amusement that even Tack, who prided himself as a connoisseur of nasty smells, took to his heels and hurried out into the fresh air.

With a dampened handkerchief round his nose and mouth Gil continued to knock away the loosening plaster, while I stood breathlessly by, waiting for the grinning skull to appear. What actually came to light, to our immense relief, were several ancient mouse nests, whose shrivelled, malodorous occupants were the cause of the assault on our nostrils. In a choking voice, due in equal parts to dust and excitement, Gil said "there's something hard here. I'm sure it's a bloody great beam. It was solid oak, beautifully curved, with the widest part off centre and narrowing towards each end of the fireplace which measured over seven feet in length. It was well weathered, and we thought it might have been salvaged from some ship long ago wrecked off the Dorset coast, and probably at the time a greatly treasured find.

We stood back, delighted with our discovery, when at that moment we heard the sound of a car coming up the lane.

"Oh no!" we wailed in unison, "not callers!"

With very few exceptions any car heading in our direction stopped at The Homestead. Mr and Mrs Potts, as far as we knew, never had visitors and, going the other way, seldom did Mr and Mrs Chatham, who lived further up the lane with their large black dog in a cottage similar to ours. Mrs Chatham boosted the budget by taking in washing for a local girls' school, and we never took our evening stroll without seeing her clothes lines groaning under the weight of a myriad pairs of brown knickers. Large ones, small ones, very small ones, long legged ones, faded and bright new first term ones, all jostling and kicking in the breeze, or dripping disconsolately leg to leg in the rain.

Our fears confirmed, the car stopped at the gate, and we stood transfixed in our dishevelment as the engine continued to run, remaining looking at each other as if in some ridiculous way we believed that if we neither moved nor breathed whoever it was would go away. There was a slam of doors, the car continued up the lane and then we heard light footsteps on the path. We looked like two fugitives from a chalk quarry. The room was filled with a fine swirling dust. There was a gaping hole above the fireplace. And there was that smell.

The footsteps halted and there, framed in the doorway, stood my younger sister Dee, paying us her first visit since our arrival at the cottage. She lived and worked as a private secretary in London, and was a town girl from her immaculate, shining shoulder length hair to her elegantly painted finger nails. She was carrying an overnight bag in one hand and a slim rolled umbrella in the other. She just said "You CAN'T live here!" and burst into tears. At that moment I was inclined to agree with her, but managed to smile gaily through the dust and, wiping my filthy hands down my filthy shirt front, urged her out into the garden, steering her gently round stoves one and two, where we sat her down in one of the chairs and managed to pacify her with a cup of tea.

To our knowledge, she was the only member of our families to have actually cried about us. The others had shaken their heads, and some had thought us ill advised to have embarked on such a venture, but all had managed to keep a stiff upper lip. My mother had kept any anxiety she may have felt to herself, for which we will always be grateful, and had even stayed a few days with us soon after moving in, putting up with the most appalling discomfort with fortitude and laughter. She was no stranger to adversity, and she simply rolled up her sleeves and got on with the job, believing strongly that any attempt by the common cold or total disaster to undermine her was an impertinence and not to be tolerated.

We were relieved when Dee, recovering though still visibly shaken, seemed pleased at the prospect of spending the weekend with us and , after changing into workmanlike shirt and trousers, she was eager to help us with the picking. With an extra pair of hands, at our insistence smothered with protective cream, we made excellent progress and carried the boxes and scales up onto the lawn where we caught up with the family gossip as we weighed and packed. Dee had been my bridesmaid, and infrequent contact by letter had kept us in touch since that day. Chatter and laughter bounced back and forth as we worked, and in no time at all the job was done and the pink, white and blue covered containers loaded into the van for tomorrow's delivery.

The sun was still warm as we sat enjoying the luxury of a glass of gin and tonic which Dee, with commendable foresight, had brought with her. The birds, all around us in the trees and hedges, were adding their repertoire of evensong to the sound of our voices. The cows, always sociable and eager to join the gathering, had moved up to the hedge and stood in an ever shifting line, thrusting their amiable heads through the gaps, eyeing us with curiosity and curling their long tongues round some fresh green morsel of supper.

We remained in the garden to eat our evening meal, watching the lapwing on the far side of the field strutting delicately, their crests bobbing, the sheen on their backs glistening green and black in the fading sun.

The air was still, and scented with roses and the pungent flowering currant as we lingered over our coffee, voices blending as the shadows lengthened, with the chorusing crickets in the long grass, and the soft splash of a tawny rat as it emerged from its deep hole in the stream bank to commence its night forage.

Chapter 6

I remember as a child reciting a poem to the effect that there were fairies at the bottom of my garden, and believed it implicitly, going often to look in the hope that one of the little people would honour me with its presence. I still like to think that it is not beyond the bounds of possibility, though most people nowadays settle for something less fanciful, like runner beans or beehives. We had neither of these at the bottom of ours. We had the privy. Squatting on the wooden topped bucket tightly enclosed by three walls and a badly fitting door was claustrophobic in the extreme, and without fail at least one eight-legged bystander would turn up despite spraying the interior with insecticide each day.

Delaying journeys of this kind tend to disturb the balance of nature, so I took to leaving the door open and feeling safely and grandly isolated until the morning I was caught with my trousers round my ankles by the new postman, who getting no reply to his knocking at the front door, had wandered round the back of the cottage in the friendly country fashion, to find someone to whom he could deliver his package.

"Morning, Mrs S," he called, not batting an eyelid, "lovely morning". Ploughing his way up through the knee high nettles, he solemnly handed me the parcel, saying "Thought I'd better find someone. You never know who's about." Too true, I thought, as red faced, I struggled with my zip, and he went on his way singing his merry postman song as if this sort of situation was a familiar part of his daily round.

Laughing about it with Gil later in the day, he said he thought it might solve the problem and be a splendid aid to concentration if we could see out, and then and there knocked a small window in the east wall overlooking the fields, and glazed it. I gave him full marks for initiative and felt inspired to give the interior a lick of paint and whitewash, long overdue, and a piece of carpet now covered the concrete floor. As a final touch of sophistication I hung a picture of the Laughing Cavalier on the door, thus ensuring that whatever it was that had amused him so uproariously in the first place, he would always have something to keep him laughing in the future.

Now we had a loo with a view and, as Gil said, one of the finest views in Dorset, and how many can boast that?

Just behind the privy grew a beautiful cricket bat willow tree, which, by its gnarled trunk which twisted in all directions, we judged to be very old. The thick branches leaned out and away, so that a kind of platform was formed in the centre, and made a perfect site for a small, low tree house. Some of its branches hung and swayed gently over the corrugated roof, its slender leaves swishing softly, a little like Titania's bower, I thought. The illusion of a midsummer idyll, however, swiftly faded in winter, when the willow creaked and groaned, lashing the hut, and icy winds blew through the crack under the door.

But that time was thankfully still ahead of us, and as August slid gently into September, it was still warm enough to sit outside grading and packing for the morning's market. One evening we continued until it was almost too dark to see, and the trees stood silhouetted black against the sky. One half of the

double garage served as a packing shed, and into this we stacked away the paraphernalia of scales, paper and boxes. We lit cigarettes, straightening our tired backs, as we listened to the sounds of the night. There was a distant murmur of traffic away up on the main road. An owl hooted in a nearby tree, and was answered seconds later by another over in the wood. A chorus of crickets made cheerful music in the bank along the stream.

Pok Pok was asleep in her tree, head tucked into wing, the beauty of the evening removed from sound and sight, and Tack was making a last inspection of the garden, his inquisitive nose alert for scent of fox or rabbit.

While I stood finishing my cigarette, thinking how lucky we were to live in such peaceful surroundings, Gil went down to the glasshouses, as he always did to "tuck up the plants". Suddenly from over by the spinney came the most spine chilling sound I have ever heard. It could only have come, I thought, from a woman being brutally murdered. I stood rooted to the spot, the hair tingling on the back of my neck. "Did you hear that?" I said as Gil came back up the path. We listened for a moment and there it was again. A blood curdling shriek ending in a gurgle. Gil calmly said he though it was a vixen.

"A vixen being brutally murdered?"

 Gil laughed and said no, he thought it might be her mating cry. It was a sound so savage and primeval that although I heard it many times in the years that followed, and learned much of the habits and character of the foxes which lived around us, it never failed to unnerve me.

It was well after eleven when we lit the lamps in the cottage, and started to prepare for bed, putting a pan of milk on the primus for our night time drink and taking it in turns to wash away the grime of the day's work. Blowing out the lamp in the living room and saying goodnight to Tack, we were startled by a loud thumping on the door, and wondered who on earth could be paying us a visit so late. Our neighbours were early to bed, and ours was always the last lamp to go out, leaving the countryside in its darkness and the nocturnal creatures to their hunting, courtship and play. Our family of hedgehogs would be snuffling and grunting its well worn way along the garden side of the stream, with or without little Willie, the smaller member. We often felt concern for Willie. That the family numbered five was certain, and on the nights when we counted only four could only, we felt, be due to his poor sense of direction, or an inability to keep up with his bustling and seemingly uncaring family. Poor Willie! We occasionally peered about with a torch to try and locate him and place him back in line, but always without success, so we left him an extra bowl of bread and milk near his home in the hedge in the hope that his sense of smell would keep him within safe bounds, and as a small consolation for having missed out on the family walkabout.

Barking furiously, Tack leapt out of his basket and flew at the door, his hackles rising. Having no telephone and it being my nature to fear the worst, whereas Gil, more positively expects and usually finds the best of a situation, my immediate thought was that some ill had befallen a member of the family, and as Gil, slipping on his dressing gown and taking the lamp from the kitchen table, unbolted the door, I held my breath as I heard him say "Yes. What can

34

I do for you?"

I saw in the soft light what appeared at first glance to be a gnome in a dirty raincoat. He had small, glinting eyes and greying stubble on his chin, and a large sack slung over his right shoulder. This he transferred to his left, and thrusting his hand towards Gil said "Boulter's the name. Boulter," with a jerk of his head in the general direction of the lane. "I thought we could have a drink," producing from his pocket a bottle of what appeared to be sherry or wine, and with such a flourish that I would not have been at all surprised to see a bunch of artificial flowers or a white rabbit.

Gil, who prefers to choose his own drinking companions, said "Not tonight, thank you," and started to close the door. Quick as a flash the gnome thrust one foot forward, and heaving the sack from his shoulder, rummaged in its depths and to our amazement brought out a violin and bow, saying "Oh well, we could have a tune, then".

With commendable restraint Gil said "We're just going to bed, so if you don't mind, some other time....", and placed himself firmly in the doorway, endeavouring to keep a frantic Tack in, and the unwanted caller out. Nothing daunted, our eccentric visitor persisted with "Perhaps I could just sketch your wife, then. A very nice lady, your wife," and whipped out of his other pocket a piece of paper and a stub of pencil, which he licked purposefully.

Scarcely able to believe the ridiculous conversation and convinced we had the local loony on our doorstep, I tried to see more of him without being seen, and realised that this was not our first encounter, and that two or three weeks previously whilst in the garden, I had heard a thud and muttered curses coming from beyond the laurel hedge. Looking over the gate I saw, a cardboard box lying on its side, spilling out what seemed like a hundredweight of small scabby apples, none other than the gnome in shambling pursuit. I ran out, and within a minute we had scooped up the runaway fruit and restored the battered box to a wooden platform strapped to the back of an ancient bicycle. With no word of thanks, and still muttering incomprehensibly, he remounted and pedalled off up the lane. Standing there watching his precarious progress, I decided that next time he found himself in such a predicament he could pick them all up himself.

And now here he was again, with a repertoire of party pieces and clearly set on performing at least one of them. By this time, Gil, quite reasonably exasperated, showed his lack of enthusiasm for the idea by taking him firmly by the collar of his raincoat, and propelled him and his sack to the gate saying "I have to be up very early in the morning. I do not want a drink, a tune or a masterpiece. GOODNIGHT". The old fellow glared balefully at him as he was moved speedily from the doorstep, and cursing and muttering "Alright, alright, ALRIGHT!" shuffled off up the lane.

For years afterwards he was to be seen pedalling erratically past, the cardboard box strapped to his bicycle, wobbling dangerously with the uneven pull of bags slung over the handlebars, but his talents having been so ungratefully rejected, he never called again.

Tack was still chuntering as he returned to his basket, and Gil was still fuming as we climbed thankfully into bed thinking, as we stretched our tired limbs, of Gil's grandmother who had insisted on buying for us, without consultation, the bed of her choice, insisting that the basis of a happy marriage was a GOOD BED.

A week before the wedding, Gil had taken delivery of the bed, and anyone could see at a glance that it would never go through the door, let alone up the stairs. Tom, Gil's brother-in-law, was with him at the time, and after earnest consultation they decided that the legs would have to come off. These unscrewed and the bed manhandled through the doorway, they found that there was no way in which the bed would go round the sharp bend in the stairs, the bed being four foot six inches wide and six feet long, and the stairs a mere two and a half feet at their widest point, with a small roughly made banister nailed into the landing at the top.

There were two possible courses of action. Send the bed back and risk offending Gil's redoubtable grandmother, or remove the banister. They decided on the more prudent course, and with a great amount of heaving and pushing and a variety of Anglo-Saxon words, it finally went through the bedroom door, came to rest against the back wall, and was then re-united with its legs.

Very soon we found that owing to the general slope towards the south, and the unevenness of the floorboards, they carried us inch by inch nearer the window, until we were driven to curb their nocturnal meanderings with Volume IV of the Encyclopaedia of Gardening under the right leg, and Volume VII and a Monica Dickens paperback under the left.

Whether it was because of our fondness for the bed, or laziness at the thought of the rigmarole of removing the legs and the banister again in order to replace it, we continued to sleep in it even though it became impossible to prevent ourselves from rolling into the middle without clutching desperately at the sides, and curvature of the spine seemed a likely result.

When, many years later, we left the cottage and finally had to part from it, it was like watching an old friend callously thrown onto a lorry and carted away to the dumping ground. As Granny Simcock had known it would be, it had been a good bed.

Chapter 7

Late September still bestowed on us the blessing of warm sun, ripening the blackberries in the hedge at the back of the cottage to glossy black, and providing us, added to the fallen apples, with delicious pies and puddings. In the shelter of the laurel hedge, the last of the roses bloomed, small and pale, and the daytime temperature in the glasshouses was high enough to ensure that the crop, though greatly diminished, was sufficient to gladden our hearts and that of our long suffering bank manager.

It seemed to us, working in our shirtsleeves, that the glorious summer was showing great reluctance to give way to autumn. The trees had scarcely begun to change colour, except for the old willow, whose slim leaves were here and there turning to a pale yellow. Knowing better, the martins had taken flight two weeks or more ago, and our resident nightingale had left to make his hazardous journey, the silence of the night a sad reminder of his absence.

The shadows of early evening came swiftly, chasing the sun's last warmth and shrouding in a low mist the darting lapwing as they made their late forage in the fields. Over by the spinney the pigeons, white against the deepening sky, played follow my leader, soaring and dipping as if by word of command round and round the tall elm, dividing and scattering like fragments in a paper chase, regrouping, soaring and dipping again and again in a glorious game.

Preparing supper one evening at this twilight time, which the local people called dimpsy, I had occasion to fetch something, now forgotten, from the storeroom, which because of the rats I preferred to visit in daylight. On opening the door, I saw a dark shape emerge from behind the old grandfather clock which stood, for want of a better place, against the back wall. The creature appeared in that brief glimpse, to be large, even for our rats, and I thought perhaps a trick of the fading light had magnified it.

I backed out quietly, cowardice triumphing over curiosity, and called Gil. We waited scarcely breathing for some minutes, warily moving one or two objects to give us a clearer view if whatever it was ran out, and I wished I had had the foresight to fetch my bicycle clips. A mouse down the neck of my shirt was one thing, but a rat up the trouser leg did not bear contemplation. There was no movement, and no sound except for the garrulous starlings settling in the thatch for the night, and our pot of tea in its bright woollen cosy was growing cold on the table, so we decided to leave the mysterious occupant in peace and have another look in daylight.

It was not until the following noon that we remembered it. Tiptoeing to the store room, we opened the door slowly and silently. Looking straight at us, too petrified to move, was a small cat. We held our breath and stood quite still, but before we could murmur a greeting, it vanished behind some packing cases, leaving us with the impression of large, round amber eyes and tabby markings on a body which was pathetically thin. We were to be denied a second look that day despite our gentle coaxing, so filling a bowl with warm milk, and breaking into it some pieces of bread, I left it just inside the door, leaving it slightly ajar.

The following morning I decided that a cycle ride to Ma Harbottle's general store up on the main road was necessary. We wanted the little cat to stay, and

keeping it well supplied with food seemed to be the first step towards establishing a relationship. Mrs Harbottle, as I remember her, was a pleasant faced lady of ample proportions who ran the store with the help of her daughter Molly, and sold a wondrous assortment of goods from sherbet dabs to shoe laces. Commenting on my purchase of cat food instead of the usual dog food, and hearing the exciting explanation, she said wisely, "It'll stay if it wants to. Don't be disappointed if when it's stronger it goes back to the wild. You can't tell a cat how to live its life.". I remember her words so well, and having shared our home with many cats over more than thirty years, can only agree with her.

For about a week I went into the store room, making certain that Tack was either shut in the cottage or in the glasshouses with Gil, since the last thing we wanted at this delicate stage was that he should chase it away, and put down food and milk, talking quietly to gain its confidence. Each time the food was taken, the saucers licked shining clean, but only when we were not about. I was taken by surprise late one afternoon, therefore, when I opened the door wide and the cat shot past me into the garden, leaping the stream and diving through the gap in the hedge. From this fastness it watched us warily, disappearing for hours at a time and always returning to the same place. I continued to call to it, placing food on a small plank which bridged the stream by the willow. Gradually it became more confident, running parellel with me along the hedge, then assuring itself that I was some distance away, treading hesitantly onto the plank to eat the food and casting nervous glances in my direction, darting back to safety at the snap of a twig.

Then the great morning came when Gil and I were talking outside the cottage door, and studiously ignoring a pair of bright eyes peering at us through the hazel branches. Gil suddenly said "I think we've got a visitor". We turned slowly round and to our immense joy we saw that the cat had jumped the stream and was standing on the path, one front paw raised, the picture of indecision. "Have I gone too far? Would it be best to turn about and head back for the hedge and safety? Or should I take the risk and introduce myself?" It's mind made up, tail waving like a flag of truce, it strolled up to us, mewing a greeting.

"It" was undoubtedly a "she", a beautifully marked young female with dark tortoiseshell stripes down her back and a delicate biscuit coloured chest. Greatly daring, and encouraged by our soft word of welcome, she allowed herself to be stroked, arching her back sharply to meet our caressing hands. Gaining confidence, she turned back and forth, rubbing gently against our legs, telling us that she was glad to meet us. We had yet to earn the accolade of a purr, but we were content, and were sufficiently confident of future visits to name her, in view of her reluctance to come into the garden, Maud.

Slowly she came to regard us as her friends, and was quite prepared to give us her companionship in the garden, but nothing would persuade her to follow us into the cottage, and I continued to leave her food on the plank for fear of rushing her into a situation she was not yet ready to accept, and breaking the slender thread of trust between us.

Tack's reaction was quite unexpected. He remained at a respectful distance, especially when the sight of him evolved furious spitting and arching of the back on Maud's part, her tail fluffing up like a flue brush. Poor Tack was jealous of the attention we paid her, and the prospect of sharing us with, of all creatures, a CAT, must have been a misery for him. We could almost read his mind. No point in inviting trouble. He could wait. And once he had her cornered high up in the apple tree he would see to it that she stayed there, and he would once more have the garden, and us, to himself.

Curiously, the fact that she took to accompanying us on our walks up the lane did not seem to worry him, possibly because outside his own territory responsibility for it and us lessened, and besides there were so many other interests to engage him. The Chathams' large black dog sitting behind his gate wagging a friendly greeting was always fair game for a barrage of insults and taunts. And the rich variety of smells, especially after rain, engrossed him fully as he zigzagged, nose to ground, from hedgerow to hedgerow to check on the movements of the local rabbit population the night before. We went in procession, Tack romping ahead, barking at us now and then to keep up. Maud sat in the middle of the road waiting for us to get well in front, then dashed past us, tail erect and ears laid back, sitting down again and repeating the whole madcap performance.

Pok Pok usually brought up the rear, walking sedately as befitted a lady of advanced years, lifting her feet high in a slow dignified goosestep, if one can apply that description to a hen. Then realising she was being left behind, all dignity forgotten, down went her head, up went her wings, and with a comical side to side scamper, she caught up with us and The Homestead squad was once more in formation.

Sometimes on reaching the end of the lane where it narrowed to a steep muddy track to Colehill, Maud, if the mood took her, declined to return with us and leapt the narrow ditch to disappear through the beech hedge, burnished to a brilliant, crisp copper in autumn and winter, which bounded Miss Lovejoy's garden. We sometimes feared that she might desert us to join the large family of waifs and strays which Miss Lovejoy took under her compassionate wing, the ground floor of her large brick house being covered, floor and furniture, with newspaper, and everywhere the smell of cooking fish.

She was a remarkable lady, a blue stocking with a lively sense of humour and hating to be idle for a moment. She lived alone in the big house, preferring her books and her garden, her chickens and her cats, occasionally numbering as many as twenty at a time. She was unable to refuse any cat arriving at her door, and was engaged in a running battle with the local authority who considered the number detrimental to health. But her big heart embraced them all, the flotsam and jetsam which came to her, lost and abandoned, mangy, old, sick timid and mistrustful, running to hide at the approach of strangers as Maud had done. She cured their ills when she could, tended their wounds, sometimes inflicted by the odious gin traps which in those days were used legally by farmers and poachers, and which today, although banned, are still claiming their pathetic victims.

Knowing no fear of intruders, although her neighbours felt uneasy on her behalf, she slept winter and summer on a narrow bed on the open verandah overlooking the back garden, which she tended with untiring fervour, impervious to weather, and seemed equally content to do so day or night, sometimes to be seen in the darkness busy in the long vegetable garden or, hurricane lamp in hand, scurrying down to shut in her chickens against marauding foxes.

We were happy that Maud, another independent spirit, was happy to make her home with us, sometimes accompanying us down the lane unseen, stalking us on the far side of the hedge, and suddenly dashing out as we reached the gate with an expression which clearly said "Here I am! That fooled you. You thought I was still up there, didn't you?"

Usually having had her fun with us, she would go off into the fields to hunt, but sometimes she sat on the path watching us as if deciding whether or not to accept our invitation to join us indoors. One evening I said, "Maud looks

41

as if she'd like to come in tonight. Why don't we try bringing her in?"

Saying "Come on, Maud, come and be sociable," Gil picked her up, something she allowed us to do without struggling out of our arms, and carrying her into the cottage, closed the door with his foot. She leapt, spitting, from his grasp, raking his arm with her claws as she did so. We had never seen such terror in an animal and were quite unprepared for the evident distress we had caused her. She backed into the walls and crawled on her stomach before, in sheer blind panic ignoring the door which had hastily been re-opened for her, she made a dash for the window. Gil managed to beat her to it and flung it open before she had the chance to injure herself.

As we saw her leap the stream and disappear through the hedge, we were stricken with remorse, and knew that we should have foreseen that she, half wild, would hate such confinement, and cursed ourselves for our unthinking foolishness, vowing that the next time she entered the cottage it would be of her own volition, with confidence and trust.

Chapter 8

As the days shortened, the fern in the spinney turned from pale rust to gold in the low rays of October sunshine, and the squirrels made haste to gather in their store of nuts. A cold wind cutting across from the east stirred the branches of the apple tree, plucking and teasing the brittle, dying leaves until they whirled and fluttered to the lawn.

We decided, as the nights grew colder, that we should take matters into our own hands and decide for Pok Pok where she should sleep, and that until the warmer weather the pear tree must be out of bounds lest one morning we should go down and find her frozen to the branches. As she had always shown such an aversion to the large henhouse, Gil set to and spent a grudging day making a small roosting house, with sloping sides of chicken wire on wooden frames, one of which contained a small door which could be left open for her during the day and replaced once she was safely tucked in at night. He put up an easily accessible perch, and covered the sleeping area with wall to wall straw. The whole job a custom built boudoir for one elderly hen.

Knowing her as we did, however, it was not unexpected that she would treat Gil's offering with contempt, hurling herself against the netting and squawking at us to let her out and back into the pear tree. After several days of ungrateful argument, we devised a variety of beds for her, far less commodious, such as a straw filled box in the packing shed, a straw nest in the store room, a wooden perch made out of an old broom handle, sawn off and stuck into a hole in the garage wall. All were rejected out of hand, until Gil lost his patience and exploded "It's absolutely bloody ridiculous! I'm not going to be dictated to by a scrawny bundle of feathers" And picking her up he dropped her none too gently into the basket attached to my bicycle which was as usual propped against the wall, saying "See how you like that!" Scolding loudly, she hopped out onto the cold chrome handle bars, where to our disbelief she settled happily, roosting there that night and every night after, one of us wheeling the bicycle and its slumbering passenger into the store room before darkness fell. Laughing ruefully, we breathed a sigh of relief that, accidentally or not, we had found something to please her, and that the pear tree seemed to be forgotten.

All went well for a week or two, but sadly her advanced years began to affect her balance and there were frequent tumbles to the ground in a squawk of ruffled feathers. Finally, she decided for herself to do what Gil had crossly suggested for her in the first place, and crooning happily, she tucked back her wings and subsided into the depths of the basket.

Not surprisingly, the basket became quite unusable as a receptacle for anything but sleeping hens, and whenever I needed the bicycle I had to unstrap it, and remember to replace it on returning with my shopping bags hanging unsteadily on the handle bars.

As an experiment I tried propping up the basked on an old table, and hanging it on a hook on the wall just inside the store room door, thinking that if the height and angle were roughly the same, she would not complain. She did, and refused to use it unattached to the bicycle, fussing and fretting and very indignant that I had dared to tamper with her bedroom. To complicate matters she began to spend less time scratching about in the garden, and more time sleeping during the day, and noisily resisted any attempt to dislodge her when I needed to go shopping.

There was only one thing to be done. I acknowledged defeat and gave up cycling in favour of walking, happy in the knowledge that she was curled up in her chosen bed, head hidden under wing, and the fit of the basket so snug round her that disorderly feathers escaped through the gaps in the cane.

We, on the other hand, were not at all snug, despite the thickness of the walls, as the persistently cold wind whined and moaned, clutching at the cottage with spiteful fingers. After all the glorious days devoted entirely to maintaining the crop, we found ourselves, like the grasshopper in Aesop's fable, ill prepared for winter, and had to set to and devise a makeshift fireplace to fill the untidy space from which stoves 1 and 2 had been ejected. The original hearth was nothing but broken brick and rubble, which Gil levelled with concrete. There were many treasures to be found on the nursery, among them a large concrete slab which we heaved into the wheelbarrow and trundled into the living room, laying it as a base for a handsome wrought iron dog grate which had been given to us by Tom's uncle. Down in the orchard we found small heaps of old bricks scattered in the long grass, and carefully selecting them for their beautiful mellow colour, bore them triumphantly up to the cottage where Gil, adding bricklaying to his hitherto undiscovered skills, edged the front of the wide hearth.

Many other articles, long buried and less useful, came to light over the years. Broken cups and plates, half a chamber pot, many gin traps, and later when we laid a pipe from the well to the cottage we were astonished to find under the path outside the front door two thirds of a bicycle, and an umbrella from which all the spokes had rotted, leaving the bone handle and the material intact. We found, too, several large tin sheets of the kind which were nailed outside shops advertising such commodities as Jeyes' Fluid, Colman's Mustard and Wills' Cigarettes, which had been used largely for propping up the sides of the stream in places where the banks were in danger of collapse, and which would probably be regarded today as collectors' items of memorabilia.

We burnt mainly wood, logs sawn from the plentiful branches which we carried and dragged back from the fields and hedgerow, reaping an extra harvest after a day or two of high winds, and assisted joyfully and noisily by Tack who liked to do his share, showing off by selecting a stick twice his size and soon tiring of his burden, dropping it for us to retrieve before scampering home ahead of us.

The day's work done, it was pleasant to shut out the night and sit in the soft yellow light from the oil lamps, stretched out luxuriously towards the fire, and moving a lazy foot to extinguish the occasional spark from the shifting logs. Flames crackled and spat in the comfortable silence and threw their darting reflections of red and orange at the copper warming pan on the far wall, and Tack rested a contented head on his front paws, back legs outstretched and occasionally twitching in the throws of some delicious dream chase.

A cosy picture, but the dog grate was a greedy master, demanding to be fed too frequently and giving out very little heat in return, most of it disappearing up the wide chimney and sometimes leaving us so cold that we were forced to sit, squaw-like, in blankets. The direction of the wind was all important, and on occasions when it shrilled like a demon from the north, we knew we were in for an uncomfortable evening, and that sooner or later the quiet intimacy would be shattered by a great roar and a belch of black smoke which filled the room, Gil commenting drily that if all other means of communication failed, we could always fall back on smoke signals.

Enveloped in a thick pall, our eyes smarting, we quite often sought refuge in the Cricketer's Arms where we could be sure of a warm welcome from a huge, well behaved fire. Unless it was one of Jethro's evenings, that is. Then the regulars knew, and the casual patrons soon learned, the advisibility of giving the fireplace a wide berth so that Jethro, who in any case regarded his place at the fire and the polished wheelback chair with its faded chintz cushion as his undisputed right, should be allowed to occupy it in splendid isolation, the reason being his long estrangement from soap and water, which as the evening wore on became increasingly noticeable, the heat from the blazing coals drawing out from the folds of his ancient army greatcoat an aroma not unlike ripe gorgonzola cheese.

An octogenarian, he did what farm work he could, still pitching a full fork of hay with the best of them, and cutting the frost covered kale at winter's first light. Like all old countrymen, he knew the fickleness of nature in all her moods and the rhythms of the seasons, reading the signs in the first pale barley shoot, in the antics of the mad March hare, in the blossom of the blackthorn and the caw of the gregarious, nesting rooks in the tall elms. He maintained that he had started on the farm on the second day of his life, carried into the fields strapped to his mother's back, for the potato lifting, and we believed him when he told us that at that tender age he could remember his mother sitting on an upturned bucket to partake of her dinner and cold tea from a bottle, at the same time deftly swinging him round from back to front so that, cradled in the crook of her arm, he too could avail himself of liquid refreshment.

It was Jethro's proud boast that he had never gone beyond the Dorset county boundary, saying "Never reckoned vureign parts, s'know. Nor vureigners neither," glaring round the bar, his bleary eyes resting briefly on those of us unable to claim Dorset beginnings. Trying to impress, I remember saying that my birthplace was Hampshire, and fairly close, to which he gave a scornful snort "Hah! 'ampshire 'og!'", and Gil, who was born in Cheshire, might just as well have come from Outer Mongolia for all the rating it gave him in Jethro's eyes.

No one remembers him buying a drink, and at closing time he left to wend his uneven way home, the money intact in his pocket, if indeed there had ever been any, his old walnut face as red as one of our tomatoes with a touch of blotch. Yet he was never seen without a pint of old and mild in his rheumaticky, soil ingrained hand. As he put it, "I likes beerr. Makes I vaart. And when I vaarts, knows I'se 'ealthy," at frequent intervals leaving no doubt in the minds of all present that his health was excellent.

45

Chapter 9

The crop which had borne us so much beautiful fruit was at an end, and the once proud gleaming trusses hung slack and yellowing on their fillis supports. The returns from the crop were good, and we felt that we had made a promising start, at the same time not allowing ourselves too much complacency, knowing that responsibility for the whole life cycle of the next crop would be ours. There would be no ready made trusses of shining leaves and healthy fruit ripe for the picking. Our income would depend solely on our own skill and care of the tiny seeds which we would have to sow in January, and feed and tend like precious infants from the time the first green shoots broke the soil.

But first the dying crop must be stripped out to make way for young lettuce when ready for planting, and the glasshouses fumigated, and while Gil consigned the limp foliage to its funeral pyre, I filled baskets with the remains of the fruit for our own use. The green tomatoes I put aside for chutney, stacking the remainder in boxes, along with the boxes of apples, on the kitchen floor, so that I could sort them into three grades - not ripe, ripe and use now. I reflected as I sorted that once they were all eaten the housekeeping budget would suffer a serious setback, and since quite often it had been a case of tomatoes or nothing rather than tomatoes with everything, I was filled with gloom at the prospect of being without our daily ration. I had dreamed up an astonishing variety of tomato based dishes, and thought perhaps I should compile a helpful handbook for wives of pioneer nurserymen on "How to live on tomatoes without turning red, round and shiny," and later, once we had acquired the necessary experience which I was certain we were about to, a second more practical volume entitled "How to avoid starvation between crops."

Our catch crop of lettuce which we had sown in October had been pricked out and would soon be ready for planting in the long double house. At this time, only the fifty foot house and the propogating house were heated by anthracite burning boilers. By the following winter, when we had installed a full heating system, we were able to extend our catch crop to chrysanthemums in pots, which greatly assisted in bridging the gap. Now, however, with little experience and a dwindling purse which must be made to stretch until the first pick of tomatoes in March, survival was the name of the game.

But now the houses must be dug over to prepare for the tiny lettuce, a task Gil enjoyed, the hard physical exercise warming him to such a degree that he was often stripped to the waist. Apart from myself, whose progress with a spade was willing but slower, Tack and Maud quite often kept him company, the latter supervising operations, sitting on an upturned box lazily washing herself and taking advantage of the watery sun which was an infrequent and welcome visitor on those grey, chill days. Tack, on the other hand, participated noisily in the undiminished hope that some delectable item, presumably a well matured bone of undreamed of proportions, would manifest itself, darting backwards and forwards in an ecstacy of anticipation. The fact that nothing more interesting turned up than an occasional piece of broken china or a surprised worm never dampened his enthusiasm, and he was always on hand when there was digging to be done.

The disinterred worms were of great interest to our other daily companion, whom we named Cheeky Chappie after Max Miller, who many will remember as a wartime comedian whose naughty eyes and flamboyant style were a source of huge merriment. Our resident robin was an opportunist and bright enough to know that if he hung about and with no effort on his part, he was in line for a substantial protein supplement to his diet, waiting for each fat worm to be thrown in his direction, snatching it up and hopping to the other side of the house to devour his ill fated, wriggling titbit. Taking a well earned break from our labours, and the inevitable interruption in his food supply met with disfavour, which he demonstrated by perching on a fork handle and chittering crossly at us until, our mugs of tea drained, Gil leapt to his feet and giving him an elaborate salute said "Sorry, Sir. Just having a break, Sir. Back on the job. Sorry, Sir." Causing Cheeky Chappie to fly up to the eaves in alarm.

Laughing, I said "He's not going to answer you, you know. He's not a budgie. I'm worried about him, Tack. He's talking to the birds again."

"Well, you're talking to the dog, so what's the difference? You talk to anything that moves."

Which was true. Naturally, daily conversations with Tack and Maud, both of whom we knew understood every word we spoke, were commonplace, and with Pok Pok when she put in an appearance, mostly in fluent HEN. Lesser creatures, especially wood lice, were frequently scolded with "Stupid Granny Pig. Come out. You'll drown if you stay in there". Or, with a helping hand, "Get off your back. I really would have thought with all those legs you could have managed to stay upright." Grubs and beetles, quite understandably reluctant to leave their chosen homes under the bark of logs, had to be warned that they were in danger of incineration on our fire, and the childhood habit of instructing ladybirds to fly away home because their homes were on fire and their children would burn lingers still, although it always seemed an unnecessarily alarming and deceitful way of telling them they would be better off somewhere else. I often mooed to the cows on my way up the garden, with very little response it must be said. Occasionally one would stop chewing the cud for a brief instant and look enquiringly at me with large brown eyes, but no answering moo came to me over the hedge.

I only ever once spoke to a spider, and that was to apologise before, in a moment of panic, I dropped a heavy book on it. I am not proud of it, and neither the spider nor the book benefited from the cowardly act.

Gil, on the other hand, preferred to talk to the plants in the belief that they will respond to the vibrations of the human voice, a theory I wholly support, which is why he was often to be heard exhorting them to "Grow, you buggers, grow!"

Leaving him to his task I went up to the garage to check on our supply of distemper, which I knew I would need for the following morning. Pok Pok joined me as I walked up the path, the keen wind comically ruffling her knicker feathers and almost blowing her off course as she progressed unsteadily, I deliberately slowing my pace in order not to overtake her. I was particularly happy to see her, as her unsociability of late, and her increasing lack of balance was causing us great concern. She no longer joined us on our walks, but she had visited the glasshouses once or twice to see what we were all up to. The soft, yielding earth, however, was not to her liking, and she preferred to stay outside on firmer ground, snoozing in the long grass and occasionally scratching about at the doorway. She still laid a few eggs, but all over the place, so that look as we might, by the time we came across then they were inedible and would undoubtedly have been considered a great delicacy by the Chinese, who I am told, prefer theirs about a hundred years old.

Pulling my jacket more closely round me, I glanced at the grey sky, where high up flocks of peewits circled, calling and swooping down in their hundreds to strut behind the slowly moving plough in Parson's field in their quest for insects, having to share the earth's bounty with the starlings and gulls which raucously and greedily snatched up more than their fair share.

It was important that the next day should be bright and dry, so that, given good light early in the morning I could smarten up our bedroom by giving the walls a second, more thorough coat of paint. Fearing a repeat of the hard lesson learned in the living room we prudently decided to wait until the spring to remove the wallpaper which, covered in its pink wash, bubbled and bulged and, to use an expression of my mother's, only fitted where it touched. No ladder would be necessary, as I could reach the ceiling, and was confident that I could cover the whole room in a day, not forgetting that by mid afternoon the light would be fading, and to paint by lamplight would be well nigh impossible. The window, with its overhanging thatch, was very small, two casements of not more than three feet in total width and about as deep, and during the long hot nights of the summer it had been difficult to sleep. Looking back on those airless nights I wonder that we did not simply pick up our pillows and take them into the garden to sleep under the stars. After all, everyone was used to the sight of us sitting out in armchairs, so they would not have been surprised to stumble upon us stretched out on the lawn in blissful slumber.

One of our customers, whom we called Mrs. Strawberry Peppermint, lived in a larger, grander version of our cottage, but with the same characteristically small windows. The reason for our name for her escapes me now, but I seem to remember that it closely resembled her own double barrelled name. It may also have been because of the loose striped garments she wore, and the strange pink tinge to her blonde hair, which these days would go quite unnoticed among the vivid oranges, greens and purples. She was a lady of Amazonian proportions, very jolly, bringing up her family with a kind of blowsy good nature, there appearing to be no Mr. Strawberry Peppermint, her untidy garden being always littered with bicycles, tricycles, animals and other peoples' children.

We knew exactly how she must have felt when, one stifling night at the height of the summer, the heat became unbearable and she became so desperate after tossing and turning for hours that she fetched from the garage a chisel and a heavy hammer, and wearing not a stitch of clothing, knocked a large hole in the cob wall. Covered from head to foot in a fine yellow dust, she collapsed exhausted on the bed and slept soundly until morning.

I could not have hoped for a better day. The sun shone and a brisk wind blew, teasing the last of the leaves from the trees. Maud, in frisky mood, chased them about the lawn, leaping high in the air and, wild eyed, skeetered past an unimpressed Tack, who had better things to do than join in the madness.

While we breakfasted we read the mail, which like everything else about that day I remember well. There were some bills, a postcard from Maurice telling us to expect him the following weekend, and a large envelope marked OPEN IMMEDIATELY, which we obediently did, to find that we had been "chosen" to enter for a GRAND DRAW, the prize for which was a villa in Spain, or perhaps it was just a holiday, provided we sent six packet tops of Brikky-Brix, or some such cereal, and stated in so many words why we liked it. Having already tried it, this ruled us out straight away as competitors, and as the winter sun streamed in through the window, slanting to touch Tack's shining back with a finger of gold, I said "Just look at it out there. Who on earth would want to go to Spain, anyway?"

Except for the bed, which was a permanent fixture, we piled the furniture on the landing wherever we could find a space which was not covered with rows of apples and tomatoes, and as I have never been a clean and tidy painter, attacking the job with more enthusiasm than finesse and ending up as well, if not better, painted than the walls, it was essential to cover everything within splashing distance with newspaper and dust sheets. Turning on the wireless and promising Gil to join him for mid morning break, I set to work.

Having said that I could not have hoped for a better start to the day, it would be difficult to have foreseen a worse end to it. Poor Gil never did have his coffee that morning, and thinking that I had become so engrossed in the job that I had forgotten the time, he came up from the glasshouses shouting up the stairs in mock severity, "I suppose I'll have to get my own coffee today. It's not good enough, You'll have to be replaced." Not receiving the expected retort, he came up to find me rocking backwards and forwards, doubled up and gasping with pain.

Statistics might show a large number of women who started the day decorating the bedroom, and ended it with a miscarriage. Fewer, perhaps, to whom pregnancy came as a total shock. My most vivid memories of that morning were of Gil's face, as white as the newly painted wall, the persistently cheerful strains of "Housewives' Choice" on the wireless, and the kindly, concerned face, closely resembling an amiable bloodhound, of a large doctor in a heavy overcoat, filling the small doorway as he edged through the piled up furniture and crossed the dust sheeted floor.

I also remember, before his arrival, my ridiculous insistence on the rug. "Put the rug down," I said, in the circumstances probably the most inconsequential remark I could have dreamed of, but which made perfect sense to me at the time. The rug, which was a cherished wedding present from a dear friend, was white with a beautiful pattern of trailing pink roses round the border, and had been carefully put away until all decorating had been completed and the bedroom deemed worthy of its presence. I can only suppose I thought there was some chance that it would lend an air of respectability to the chaotic scene. Gil, his shocked expression changing to one of amazement, and no doubt thinking that I had taken leave of my senses but deciding it would be best not to argue, fetched the rug from its layers of paper, rolling it out beside the bed where it lay as pure and incongruous as a sunbeam on a rubbish tip.

Like all young couples, we had discussed the possibility of children, and had agreed that for the time being, struggling as we were to establish ourselves, and with the lack of amenities in the cottage, a family must come very low on our list of priorities. So that when Maurice arrived two days later and said, outrageously misquoting Oscar Wilde's Lady Bracknell, "To lose a child can be counted a misfortune. To loose a child one didn't know one had looks like carelessness," we laughed, but could only agree with him, and could have added and crass stupidity too.

The District Nurse, Sister Dorey, made daily visits. She was a short, stout lady with an ample bosom on which her fob watch lay horizontally, thus saving her the trouble of lifting it to read it. She crackled with starch, was bossy, was fond of using the royal "WE", meaning me, and remarkably devoted to the efficacy of enemas, an enthusiasm I did not share. Her cluckings, as she bustled about, and her easily ruffled feathers put us in mind of Pok Pok on one of her difficult days, but provided we did as we were told the atmosphere remained cordial, and she even allowed herself an occasional little hum as she went about her tasks. We were grateful for her ministrations, and when I thanked her and apologised for the conditions which must have made her job more difficult, saying that perhaps in the circumstances things had turned out for the best, she looked at me reproachfully saying "Good gracious! I've delivered babies in far worse places than this!"

Looking fondly round the lopsided little bedroom, temporarily restored to order, the rose patterned curtains once more at the window, and with one and a half walls of pristine white, two and a half pink, I could believe her, and as I drifted off to sleep I glanced towards the cradle nook, in deep shadow beyond the radius of soft light from the lamp on the dressing table, and said softly, "Sorry, Nanny. Better luck next time."

Chapter 10

For several months we had been laying siege to the Electricity Board, having noticed on our walks up the lane that there was a transformer on the telegraph pole opposite Miss Lovejoy's house, which meant three things. That she had electricity, that it had been brought down from Colehill, and that if we played our cards right there was a chance that we could persuade the Board to extend the supply to us, a distance of about a quarter of a mile, the Chatham's cottage being situated somewhere about halfway between.

We had great hopes that this would be our first and last winter necessitating the use of oil, any romantic notions we may have held about oil lamps having vanished with the sheer inconvenience of filling and cleaning and moving them about from place to place according to whose need was greater, and the novelty of creeping up the little wooden stairs to bed, candle in hand like Wee Willie Winkie, had by now lost its appeal. We were also nervous about the safety aspect of the use of paraffin under a thatched roof, as judging by the enormity of the premium we were asked to pay, was the company with whom we were insured. To us the possibility of an electricity supply would mean not only light, both domestically and in the glasshouses, and cooking without the use of paraffin and primus stoves, but most importantly, it would mean that a pump could be attached to the well, and the water piped up to the cottage.

On the face of it, it seemed to us perfectly simple. But, as we discovered, nothing is simple to what Gil calls the pettifogging bureaucratic mind, and our requests and applications went unheeded, the only reason given being that extending the supply was not in the Board's programme for the foreseeable future. They had reckoned without Gil. As a Cancerian he can show crablike and tenacious characteristics, and was in no mood to let go. A believer in the theory that if one wanted something done one should start at the top, he jumped into the van and drove to the Head Office in Bournemouth, where he received the same disinterested reply.

Regarding this setback as purely temporary, he retreated to remuster his forces, and a week or so later was once more on his way to Bournemouth, where I gather he gave the dramatic performance of his life. He was the ex-service man who had "done his bit" for his country, and was struggling to re-establish himself in civilian life, working his socks off to make a living, with a hungry wife to feed, and when he was seeking to better the conditions in which we were living and increase our income to above starvation level, he had come up against a wall of feeble excuses and prevarication. That was the gist of it. Whether it was the sheer eloquence of Gil's delivery which pierced the grey suited armour of the man at the top, finding beneath a soft heart and sympathy for our cause, or whether utter weariness at the prospect of further wordy bombardments by this persistent and obstreperous young man, we shall never know, but the Board agreed to give our request its consideration, only, to make it worth extending the supply, if we could assure it that other residents in the lane shared our desire for electricity, thus deftly throwing the ball back in our court, and probably hoping that would be the last they would hear of us.

At that time we had not met the "other enders", but set out to canvas each household, and found that a sufficient number, with the exception of Granny

Watts, were in favour of the scheme, and willing to share the cost of the operation which was to be in the region of £600.

Granny Watts, who was perfectly content with the candles and oil lamps of her childhood and saw no reason to change the tenor of her ways, spent a great deal of her time bent double in her quest for plants with which to make her wines. Nothing escaped her searching eye and acquisitive fingers. Elder blossom, cowslips, dandelions, nettles, all were plucked and consigned to various bags she carried with her wherever she went, one being reserved for firewood, twigs from the hedgerows and pine cones, and all carried up the long hill from the main road in blizzard or summer heat. Sometimes Gil drew up alongside her on his way home and earned her smiling and puffing thanks as she climbed into the van with her load for the rest of the journey, the sweet smell of the flower heads mixing strangely with the damp wood and the rubbery mustiness of her dripping, ankle length raincoat, wet weather being no deterrent to her enthusiasm.

It was a long steep hill for one of any age, low banks on either side dropping away to common land, and covered in summer with tall, creamy cow parsley, ragged robin and bladder campion, affording no shade to the weary homecomer. Nor were there any trees to lessen the bite of the wind in bleak winter. Recently we returned to Wimborne, and were pleased to find that they had been allowed to grow uncurbed, and the lane was lined on either side with elders, alders and straight young oaks, and here and there hawthorn and shimmering larch grew tall and close, casting their shade upon us as we walked, a comfort which was denied to us fifty years ago.

At the fork where we turned off sharply up the lane to the cottage, is an old brick and cast iron railway bridge which straddles the old line from Poole to Salisbury. On reaching it we found the line disused, overgrown and neglected, and instead of shining tracks, thick black mud lay like a river bed. Nature had reclaimed the line, and brambles and nettles covered the banks once dotted with primroses and celandine in spring. On one side further up the line, someone had bought part of the track, turning it into a miniature farm and smallholding, with a few cows and chickens and tumble down shacks.

As we leaned on the railings and peered over, the birds sang undisturbed, and a rabbit hopped under the bridge and away from us, its white scut bobbing and flashing in the bright sun. We were remembering the trains which had passed underneath several times a day, small friendly trains which, unlike their diesel offspring hurtling along in brash haste through the countryside, seemed in no particular hurry to reach their destination, yet arrived with unfailing punctuality. Walking up the main road, we often timed it so that if we saw one chugging towards us in the distance, we hurried up the hill and positioned ourselves on the bridge in time to receive a grimy faced grin and a cheery wave from the driver, which filled us with childish delight, before he disappeared through the brick archway and rattled off into the distance, leaving us enveloped in a billowing swirl of smoke.

If Tack was with us, which he invariably was, we made certain that he was firmly attached to us as the sight of the approaching train amused him as much

53

as us, and ears pricked forward, he would push his head through the railings, barking his greeting and leaning out at a death defying angle. Gil teased me when I took the precaution of tightening his collar, but knew that I was remembering another Pembroke corgi named Briggie, who had been my friend and constant companion during much of my service life. There was only one place where he was forbidden to accompany me. On parade. It did occur to me to put him forward as Regimental Mascot, in which case he would have been perfectly within his rights to be there, but since he did not measure up in stature to the imposing Irish wolfhound or goat so favoured by regiments there seemed little chance for him. Had he been either, of course, he could not have slept on my bed, which Briggie did every night to warn, with his built-in enemy aircraft detection system, of danger. Stationed at that time on the South Coast, known as "Buzz bomb Alley" and in a direct line from the German V.1 Rocket launching pads, I learned to wake at his first rumbling growl, feeling reasonably safe so long as he went on growling. But the moment the growling stopped and he leapt off and under the bed, that was my cue to join him until the chilling drone of the pilotless machine had continued on its way, to cut out a few miles away and plummet to its destruction and that of those unfortunate enough to be in its evil path.

What I could not know, of course, as I skulked in cowardly trembling under the bed, was that a few years hence I would marry one of the intrepid pilots whose duty it was to pursue and blow those machines out of the sky. Gil has since told me that the V.1 Rockets flew low, at between five hundred and a thousand feet, and that their speed was sometimes greater than that of his Mosquito, which made it necessary to patrol at about ten thousand feet in order to pick up sufficient speed to dive in and destroy his target. To him the sight and sound of these sinister robots moving inexorably across the sky, flames shooting from their tails, was far more eerie than any manned aircraft.

Having survived some of Hitler's nastier gifts to Britain, Briggie came very close to losing his life on a railway station en route to a new posting in Essex. I have now no recollection of which station it could have been. I can only remember vividly the horror of the occasion. Alighting from the train laden with luggage, Briggie's lead in one hand, I had great difficulty in negotiating the tremendous gap between footboard and platform, and looked in vain for a helping hand at an hour in the morning when there were few fellow passengers apart from a handful of factory workers on early shift and a sprinkling of service personnel, a porter being a rare sight in wartime. One moment Briggie was there about to jump down with me. The next I was holding a lead with nothing on the end but an empty collar, and he was underneath the hissing monster from which poured clouds of scalding steam. Someone produced a porter out of nowhere, and the sickness in my stomach was not lessened when he looked gravely at me saying "I don't give much for his chances, Miss. There's a three thousand volt line the other side." I could neither see nor hear Briggie, but I knew, if he had not already panicked and fled, that I had to try and keep him near.

A small knot of people gathered to stare at the sight of a demented woman lying full length on the platform shouting at a train. Any word that came into my head, "RATS!" "WALKS!" I shrieked into the hissing steam, hoping that something might penetrate his terror and keep him on my side of the track.

Just as I was beginning to despair of seeing him again, the porter said "I'll see what I can do, Miss," and to my undying gratitude lowered himself on to the line and went in search of a frightened, collarless little dog, As we all stood waiting in silence, a woman with her hair tied up in a scarf said, "Don't take on, love, He'll turn up. Stubborn little buggers, them Gorkies."

After what seemed hours, but was in fact a few seconds, the porter handed him up by the scruff of the neck, wet, grimy and struggling indignantly, but miraculously none the worse for his adventure. I sat on a suitcase hugging him to me, while the kind lady went to fetch me a "good strong cup of tea with plenty of sugar for shock" when really what I could have done with was a double brandy and a good cry. There, for a moment or two, sat a member of His Majesty's forces whose British backbone had turned to jelly, and whose upper lip was not stiff but trembling. And who was not ashamed of it. Briggie had shown the world that it would take more than Hitler and Southern Railways combined to quench his indomitable Welsh spirit. There was only one thing which concerned me at that moment, and that was the look on the face of my new Commanding Officer, to whom I was about to report, my best uniform covered from shoulder to hem in thick soot, my hair tumbling out of its customary neat roll, and a large hole in the knee of one khaki stocking.

Chapter 11

Gil stood in his muddy gumboots leaning on the kitchen sill, tea mug in hand, listening intently to the wireless. Drops of rain fell unheeded from the thatch onto the shoulder of his old leather jerkin, and gleamed like teardrops in the fading winter light on the bare branches of the hedge.

"You don't think Sally's really going to do it, do you?"

"Well, we'll have to wait until tomorrow to find out", Gil said gravely, draining his mug and stumping off back to check on his sweet peas before darkness fell. Like me, he was earnestly taken up with our daily dose of Mrs. Dale's Diary, A B.B.C. saga of middle class suburbia in which Mrs. Dale always seemed to be worried about Jim, her doctor husband, who worried about his mother in law, Mrs. Freeman, who worried incessantly about her cat, Captain. This teatime drama was something we would not have missed for the world, and if there was work to be done elsewhere, the wireless went with us.

"The Archers," too, provided us with our evening entertainment, just as it does still for millions of listeners. Simplicity of storyline and dialogue was the keynote of the programme, and the characters, "country folk" all, were credible enough to involve us in their dilemmas and squabblings to the extent of arguing for and against on some situation which had arisen. Many will remember the death of Grace Archer as a black day indeed, and the story goes that so many were devastated by her untimely removal from the script that on the day of her "funeral" wreaths by the hundred were received at Broadcasting House. Although not gullible in that sense, nevertheless we were shocked by the callousness of the scriptwriters, and wore mournful faces for days, only just restraining ourselves from wearing black armbands as a mark of respect.

Nowadays, though still a story of country folk, modern farming methods, political changes, sociological problems, the whole spectrum of life fifty years on, have given the programme a sharpness and sophistication with all its topicality, that in our naivety we would have found hard to accept.

Gil's sweet peas, which were his own idea and of which he had every reason to be proud, were being attacked by mice. Not only were they still active in the cottage, but now they were systematically stealing his babies, and that could not be allowed to continue. He had sent away for some expensive, high quality seed, and had planted them out in a hundred and fifty pots which, among other treasures, we had come across in the long grass behind the small house, putting them in the cold house. Within two days every pot had been plundered, and each time he sowed more, the seed was stolen.

Having nothing personal against mice, but determined that the situation must be dealt with, he made a wooden box with glass on one side. Whether this was so that he could see in or the culprit see out was never established. At one end was a hinged door with a spring, which could be held up by a catch. Inside the box was a small cup which held the bait, one or two seeds, and the idea was that when the mouse entered, down came the flap, thus imprisoning the thief. It worked. The first morning when he went down to check, he found a frantic little creature, well fed but ungratefully demanding to be let out.

Gil, too soft hearted to dispatch it, and remembering the trauma of the trap, obliged by carrying the box into the field and setting it free. This turned out to be a wrong step, as it came back with its friends, and as he sowed more seed, so they were dug up out of the pots.

Once more the grey matter was brought to bear, and he built a platform on which he placed the pots, suspending the whole contraption from the roof of the house. Our mice had proved themselves to be an athletic species, but they were defeated when it came to jumping three feet for their breakfast, and all the plants survived, and were later planted out under cloches, producing a magnificent crop the following May.

Mrs. Freeman was not the only one who was worried about her cat. As the weather worsened and the wind cut across from the east, whipping the bare branches of the apple tree into gnarled witch fingers, and pushing at the window panes in its fury, we wished with all our hearts that Maud would join us in the cottage, but knew better than to persuade her. She would do so in her own time. We knew that she hunted by night, disappearing through the hedge into the fields, and depositing the results of her activities, small mangled remains of mice and voles, in the garden, We could only ensure that there was somewhere warm and snug for her to sleep if she so desired, and were content in the knowledge that she quite often shared the store room with Pok Pok, curled up in the depths of a cardboard box in the folds of Gil's old jumper, always making certain that the door was propped open a few inches to allow for her comings and goings.

Slumped, on such a night, in soporific ease by the fire, it was tempting to postpone the late last call of nature, but if obedience was unavoidable, the chilly trek to the privy was not too tiresome if I ran there and back, swinging the torch in a wide arc over the path ahead, and taking in my stride the loud snap of a twig, the eerie hoot of an owl, or the scurrying of something disturbed by the light, telling myself that the sudden cough from the other side of the hedge is only a bronchial cow, silly.

Maud would often greet me along the way, appearing from nowhere with a cheerful chirrup, all things of darkness familiar and exciting to her and holding no terrors. On one such night when the icy rain hurled against the cottage walls, and no creature should find itself without shelter, I prepared to bid my escort goodnight, saying as I always did, "Is it going to be tonight, Maud? Coming in?

Opening the door and dashing shivering into the welcoming warmth, I paused, reluctant to close the door on Maud, who was standing irresolutely, eyes slitted against the rain, her wet fur clinging to her small body. Suddenly, to my astonishment, she skeetered through the door, shaking the rain from her paws with a comical hop and a skip. Realising the enormity of the step she had taken she froze as if to stone, and it looked as if she would repeat her panic flight.

As we held our breath, her eyes went to the fire and she slowly moved towards it as though hypnotised by the leaping flames, pausing to lower a dainty twitching nose to Tack as he lay asleep on the rug. Then began a lengthy and thorough washing. Scarcely able to believe what was happening, we pretended to continue with our reading, the silence broken only by the shifting and spitting of the burning wood. Her ablutions completed to her satisfaction, she sat motionless, watching the fire with unblinking eyes, the ancient cat, mysterious, fathomless, her thoughts a private matter. All at once, her mind made up, she turned her head and looked at me for a moment, then walked purposefully towards my chair. I said "Hello, Maud," and with an answering chirrup she sprang lightly onto my lap, turned round several times, and purring loudly as I began to stroke her soft back, curled herself up as if she had always been there, and slept.

Chapter 12

Impossible, now, to recognise the fields and spinney as those which, during the glorious summer months blazed with vibrant colour and shimmered with heat, the now dreary landscape relieved only by the occasional burst of scarlet from the hops in the hedgerows and the glint of orange rust as the winter sun pointed a pale finger at the shrivelled bracken.

In the garden, the last fallen leaves had vanished, and a solitary marigold lingered defiantly with the bronze chrysanthemums in the long bed by the laurel.

Birdsong had diminished, the birds giving all their attention to survival and, like prima donnas, saving their voices for their big performance in the spring. The blackbird alone seemed not to have noticed the cold rain dripping on his head through the branches, continuing with his cheerful chorus, to be rewarded with a handful of raisins and any stored apples that were found to be deteriorating. Pulpy, brown and slushy, they were all the same to him and he pecked at them on the lawn with great enthusiasm. Catering for all tastes, we hung a nutbag on the apple tree for the tits, and were amused to see how adept the sparrows had become at copying them, hanging upside down and pecking out the nuts efficiently. We scattered grated cheese under the laurel for the wrens, the most delightful songsters of the small birds and sadly reduced in numbers thanks to insecticides.

"We can't afford to feed this lot," grumbled Gil. "They're eating better than we are."

Not far from the truth. We were certainly counting every penny until the next crop, which meant a cheap and cheerful diet, our greatest standby being knife and fork soup, as we called it because it was so thick with lentils and vegetables that it was almost impossible to eat with a spoon, and eaten with bread and cheese or jacket potatoes, delicious. The few remaining tomatoes and apples on the landing were almost gone, and once I could no longer include them in the menu, I thought there would be nothing for it but to climb up the apple tree and fight it out with the birds, but fate smiled on us in the shape of one of our wholesalers who sent his driver out with his lorry asking for lettuce. Ours were still small and unhearted, but the demand, with Christmas on the horizon, had exceeded the supply and they were desperate enough to offer us a price out of all proportion to their maturity.

Enthusiastically we set to and boxed them, a few days later receiving a cheque for a sum far in excess of the normal price we would have expected for full grown lettuce. So we and our bank manager were happy again, and we were able to go back onto solids for the next month.

Now we had only the sweet peas and the tomato seedlings in the propagating house to worry about, the small boiler needing constant coaxing and cosseting to maintain the required temperature.

The first time that Gil lit up, the house was immediately filled with black smoke, which could only mean an obstruction in the ten foot flue pipe. Climbing a ladder and peering into its depths he discovered a birds nest about a foot down from the top, which seemed an unlikely place to build, and he remembered having seen a pair of blue tits soon after we arrived at the cottage busily flying back and forth.

Gil was fortunate not to feel the cold, but I scurried about in extra jumpers, his and mine, mittens and his old (holey) socks, thinking fondly of my despised army vests of thick, serviceable wool, which together with other items of issued underwear, including three pairs of khaki bloomers, known to all as passion freezers, were frumpy objects of scorn and only saw the light of day when laid out on the bed for Kit Inspections. These weekly occurrences, which I later found to be as boring when one was doing the inspecting, were a source of great aggravation to me. There always seemed to be some item which I could not find, and the toes of my thick lisle stockings were full of holes, my sisters and I never having been taught to mend anything. I remember the inspecting officer unrolling them and saying "Why have these not been mended?"

"I'm sorry, Ma'am," I said blithely, "We don't darn as a family." With a look which wiped the smile off my face and brought me rigidly to attention, she said "I don't want to know how you were dragged up. I want to see these stockings darned. You can do it on your next two late passes."

There was now no need to worry that Maud was left out in the cold, as she came and went as she pleased, sleeping indoors quite often, and we knew that when she deserted us at night it was from choice, that domesticity now and then palled, and she wanted once more to be wild and free and off across the fields on some private business.

Thanks to her, we were no longer troubled with mice in the cottage. The word had got round on the rodent grapevine that this was no longer a safe house. She had proved to be an efficient mouser, meeting out death swiftly and cleanly, without the preliminary cruelty of tossing and teasing natural to some cats. Life in the wild had taught her, perhaps, that hunger was a stark and urgent reality, and there was no time for subleties. Now, having killed, she had no need to eat the barely marked little corpse, but brought it to us, laying it at our feet as a gift of love.

What precious gift
Could fail to move
And melt the heart
As all or part
Of a mouse in your shoe
Tucked in the toe
Just to show
It's only for you.

The rat population, too was slowly diminishing from the store room, although there were still a number making their homes in the bank alongside the stream. Sleek, tawny, bold enough to come out and sit on the bank washing their whiskers in broad daylight. Maud would sit for hours watching, immobile, poised to pounce at the slightest movement, occasionally amusing herself by dabbling a languid paw at a leaf or twig as it sped along in the fast flowing water. Tack thought his way was better - barking loudly, dancing along the bank and chasing the rats back into their holes - and a great deal more fun.

The antipathy between them lessened daily, and most evenings they shared the rug by the fire, stretched out top to toe in companionable slumber. They also fed together, which was a little unfair to Maud, as Tack's one aim was to empty his dish speedily so that he could edge her out of the way and start on hers, burping loudly and gulping greedily, a four legged waste disposal unit.

Tack was still unable to share with her our affection, and if he thought that our attention to her had gone beyond acceptable bounds, he would stage a counter attraction such as throwing himself onto his back and feigning dead, or fetching his ball and tossing it high in the air growling fiercely, which he knew always made us laugh. If that failed, he would solicit our sympathy by simply holding up a front paw which some months before had been slightly injured on a thorn, and was now perfectly healed. It never failed. We always responded with coos and sympathy, which was the desired reaction. His jealousy appeased and assured once more of our love, he trotted happily off, all well with his world.

Sadly, at that time, there was a decision to be made about Pok Pok. She now slept almost all her days, having to be lifted, without her usual scolding, into her basket at night. She was no longer able to walk to the door for her breakfast, and we carried her into the kitchen each morning, but she could not maintain her balance and toppled to one side as she tried to peck at her dish, a sight which filled us with misery.

We knew full well what must be done, but also knew that we could not be the ones to do it. We went to see Jack Haines, a kindly man who had kept chickens all his life. He told us the gallant old hen had simply come to the end of the road, and that it would be a kindness to put an end to her restricted, and for all we knew, painful existence. Knowing he was right, still we hesitated and agonised about the when the where and the how, until a few mornings later I went to fetch her in for breakfast, and found her, head tucked into wing, her blue lidded eyes closed in sleep.

It was as if she had grown impatient with our indecision, and with her customary independence had taken matters into her own hands. We buried her under her beloved pear tree, the lofty perch from which she had so loudly complained of our interference, and remembered her with affection and laughter.

How could we forget when to remind us every now and then a small brown feather lay in the long grass in the orchard, caught up in the hedge or carried joyously on the wind, twirling and soaring upwards in a merry dance until lost from sight.

Chapter 13

"There's lots of horrid belly," I said, coming through the door with an armful of berried holly.

"You've done it again," said Gil, by now used to my spoonerisms, which now and then came out of the blue, unrehearsed and unbidden, not so much a slip of the tongue as a slip of the brain.

The important thing, however, which prompted the remark, was that we thought ourselves lucky to have any holly at all. In the back garden, near the lane, was a beautiful tree, its dark shining branches ablaze with scarlet, with which we planned to deck out the cottage. A circlet of holly, ivy and red ribbons already hung on the front door, and the beams in the living room were about to receive their share of Christmas finery.

The day before, on going out to fetch some food from the safe, in winter as efficient as any refrigerator, I was startled to find a woman in a long skirt and with dark hair coiled over her ears, standing inside the back entrance lopping off large branches of holly with a pair of secateurs.

"I suppose you know this is private property?".

The woman ignored me and continued adding to the pile of holly on the ground beside her. The nerve of it!

"I said......." I started to say when from the far side of the hedge came a voice saying "No good talkin' to 'er, Missus. Deaf as an 'addock. The owner of the voice, a small man carrying a murderous looking billhook, appeared in the gateway.

"Right,! I said furiously, I'll say it again. You are on private property, and this", pointing dramatically, "is a private holly tree."

He stood looking at me with black, boot button eyes in a mean, dirt ingrained face, rubbing a calloused thumb along the blade, and I wished Gil would come up from the glasshouses.

Sounding more convincing than I felt, I said "Take what you've cut and leave or I'll call the police," fully aware that he had only to look about to satisfy himself there were no telegraph wires to be seen, and must have known that a policeman on the beat was not a usual sight in the lane.

To my relief he nudged the woman roughly, and picking up the holly walked away muttering, "Only trying to make a living, lady." I watched as they approached a van parked farther up the lane, and already loaded to the doors, and drove off.

"They're now going to sell OUR holly to the neighbours," I said indignantly.

"Damned diddycoys," said Gil. "Why didn't we think of that?"

We were greatly looking forward to Christmas, partly because we would be together for the first time in our own home, which in itself was cause for celebration, and for both of us too many festive seasons had been spent away from home and family. Gil recalls dreary spells at readiness on bleak airfields when sobriety and boredom were the order of the day, or catching up on sleep after nights of enemy activity.

As much of my service was with anti-aircraft batteries, my memories are mainly of large, cold, requisitioned houses, mostly rather grand, situated miles from anywhere, their remoteness making it necessary for an oddly assorted bunch of people to make their own fun. One in particular comes to mind of the carved minstrels' gallery hung with home made paper chains and cardboard cutouts of Father Christmas pinned to the beautiful Adam fireplace.

This year too, apart from a visit to my parents on Christmas Day, my father's illness being great cause for concern to us all, we would not be seeing friends or relatives. We could not go to them as the young plants could not be left for any length of time, and the standard of warmth, comfort and convenience we could offer any guests we might have liked to invite for the holiday was minimal. It would be a stalwart friend indeed who would have undergone the rigours of stripping off and performing ablutions in a freezing kitchen with a stone floor. In fact had it not been for the kindness of Jack and Edith Haines in allowing us the use of their bathroom every Friday I would have seriously considered giving up washing for the winter, and adopting the time honoured tradition of the gypsies, who wrapped their children for the duration of the winter in brown paper and goose grease until the spring, by which time I imagine, depending on the number of children per square foot of living space, the atmosphere would have been quite rich.

We were particularly happy, therefore, when Maurice, a hardy character and familiar with the stripfreeze, came for the weekend prior to returning to his wife in London for the holiday. As always, he worked like a beaver, sawing a pile of logs, enjoying the physical exercise after a week of inactivity sitting at his desk, and cheerful strains of "God rest ye, merry gentlemen" came floating back to us as he laboured. We made two treks to the spinney, dragging back fallen branches, filling sacks with kindling which lay thickly on the ground after the strong winds, and on the second journey stole a small spruce tree.

Tack had a wonderful time, putting up a rabbit and chasing it round and round a tree until we were of the opinion that the rabbit was chasing Tack. It could so easily have outrun him, so it was reasonable to suppose that it was having fun until, losing interest in the game, it shot through the hedge into a field of cabbage and was lost from sight in the tall leaves.

Having howled and puffed and wept through most of its span, December had decided to put on a smiling face for its remaining days, and the weather was crisp and clear with the promise of early frost. As we walked up the farm track alongside Parson's second field we were cheered by the sight of a few brave catkin tails hanging in the bare hedgerow, and chickweed, dotted like small white stars along the bank gleamed bright and cheeky in the winter sunshine.

We made toast by the fire on our return, exhilarated by the cold air and exercise, and red faced from the heat thrown out by the logs, then we drove Maurice to the station to catch his train. Not until we went up to bed did we find lying on the camp bed a bottle of brandy and a box of chocolates, with a card which read:-

> For two nice people, hoping it'll
> Express my thanks for bed and vittles.
> Happy Christmas. M.

We woke on the morning of Christmas Eve to see Maud looking out of the bedroom window gnashing her teeth at the birds. When we said "Good morning," she answered with a chirrup and jumped onto the bed, kneading and purring to ensure that we did not go off to sleep again. The sun was shining, there were birds to be put to flight, it was breakfast time, and anyway she just wanted to be let out, so would we kindly get up, please?

She seldom joined us in the bedroom, but when she did decide on it, she waited until we had got into bed before making a dramatic entrance, coming through the door at a gallop and leaping onto the bed. We were always treated to the same performance and knew exactly what to expect. Marching purposefully up the bed towards us, she fixed us with her gaze and sat down on our books until we acknowledged defeat and turned out the lamp. Then in the darkness the stomping and kneading began, accompanied by deafening purrs, until satisfied that all was now prepared for her night's rest, she curled up on the back of my neck or full length along Gil's chest, her nose a whisker's breadth away from his.

We put up with this, knowing that after a short time she would move to the bottom of the bed, where she curled up on our feet and slept, unmoving, until morning. Gil obediently got out of bed, and went downstairs to pump life into the primus stove, while I spent a few luxurious minutes pretending that at the sound of a discreet cough I should open my eyes to see Jeeves standing deferentially at the bedside with my breakfast tray and morning papers.

No such delight manifested itself, so there was nothing for it but to get up and feed the three hungry mouths waiting for me in the kitchen, and then I could concentrate on that delightful occupation, decorating our appropriated tree, which stood potted and waiting on the window sill.

From the moment I started unwrapping the glass balls Maud decided that this was solely for her benefit, and with waving tail and wild eyes shining with excitement, she started patting them round the floor and with a hefty swipe knocking them from the branches.

"MAUD! Do you mind? It's going to take me all day at this rate."

"It's her Christmas too," said Gil, engrossed in sticking two halves of a log together. This was our Yule log, willow, and hard as rock, and I had said I wanted it hollowed out to take cumpled chicken wire. After consideration Gil decided this could prove difficult as he had no suitable tools for the job.

"Can't you just scoop it out?" I asked, dismissing the problem with a simple suggestion.

Gil shot me a withering look. "What with? A spoon?"

The only solution he could think of was to saw the log down the middle lengthways and chip out corresponding hollows, which when restuck formed a deep trough into which I placed the wire. I arranged five tall red tapers along its length, filling the surrounding wire with sprigs of holly. When lit it was a beautiful and romantic table centre, and was used again and again for years afterwards. When finally the peeling bark, which was stuck back many times, was beyond repair, it was sprayed with gold, and we still have it somewhere.

"Has it occurred to you," I said, plucking Maud out of the cardboard box, "that in nativity scenes you only ever see the traditional donkey, sheep and cow. there must have been hens scratching about in the straw, cats to keep down the mice and dogs to guard, and catch rats."

"I don't know about dogs and hens, but there were certainly cats before Christ because they were worshipped as gods by the ancient Egyptians, and anyone who harmed one was put to death. Then their status dropped a bit after the coming of Christianity."

I said I was sure that I had read somewhere about an Italian legend which says that the moment Mary gave birth to Jesus, a cat in the stable had a litter of kittens, and that Leonardo de Vinci included a cat and kittens in some of his studies of the Madonna and Child. A charming story, which if true, probably accounted for the superior expression on most cats' faces, and perfectly justified in the light of their illustrious ancestry.

"Tack, wake up. do you realise this is your second Christmas?"

So far he had taken no interest in proceedings, so I presumed he was unimpressed if aware of the fact, but he must have known that this day was not as others since there was a blazing log fire roaring up the chimney, which normally would never be lit during the week before teatime, and was stretched out on the rug oblivious to Maud's madness, even when she rushed up to him and gave him a playful pat on the nose to let him know, dull old stick that he was, that he was missing an exciting morning.

Tack and I had met exactly a year before, when Gil casually said "Turn round and close your eyes. I've got a surprise for you."

He disappeared out to the car and on his return told me I could look now. This I obediently did and saw nothing until I heard a slight squeak and felt something soft brush against my ankle. I looked down to see a small, round, wriggling biscuit coloured ball of fur, around whose neck was a red ribbon bow and a large label which read "MY NAME IS TACKLEWAY COBBER. HAPPY CHRISTMAS MUM."

Like Briggie, who had died the previous year, he was a Pembroke corgi, and Gil hoped that his introduction into my life would help to lessen my sadness. At the time of Briggie's death I was working near Salisbury, a residential job which forbade the keeping of animals, and he was living with my parents in Lulworth, a mutually loving arrangement. I knew he was happy although I missed him, and our periodic reunions were joyous. We went for ong walks, searching the pebble beach for driftwood, gathered mushrooms in the fields at first light before the sea mists had lifted from the village, and climbed Bindon Hill, Briggie beating me to the top, where we sat to recover our breath before the descent, and watched the wheeling, screaming seagulls overhead.

When he became ill, in response to a telelphone call from my mother, I went home for the weekend, and as he raised his head to greet me I knew that we were meeting for the last time. I stroked the beautiful ears the colour of burnished beech in autumn and said goodby to my beloved friend.

As I travelled back to Salisbury, my sole companion in the carriage was a workman in blue overalls who stared out of the window, embarassed to see the tears which fell unchecked onto the blurred print of my morning paper.

And now there was Tack, quite a different personality, still very young, exciteable and restless, to enrich our lives with his loving and mercurial nature, and still fast asleep before the fire, until a knock at the door startled him awake and sent him hurtling doorward barking fiercely. The post came twice a day. Our usual postman Dave in the morning, and now in late afternoon a fresh faced youth weaing a G.P.O. armband who, having delivered a parcel stood hopping from one foot to another until he blurted out that he would be greateful to use our convenience, a misnomer if ever there was one. We pointed him in the direction of the back garden, Tack accompanying him all the way, having noted the lack of uniform and decided that as an unfledged postling he should be accorded a visitor's welcome, which included a chummy squeeze into the privy.

"Funny dog, isn't he?" said the lad as he returned, grinning. "Just sat there, wagging his tail."

We apologised and felt that such tolerance of Tack's eccentricity should not go unrecognised, and gave him a glass of Granny Watt's black currant liqueur, pressing into his other hand a two shilling piece and a mince pie. A cheerful whistle floated back to us as the rear light of his bicycle disappeared down the lane, zigzagging slightly, a fair indication that the kick in Granny Watt's brew was well up to standard.

We had been the happy recipients of several such brews, neatly labelled and delivered by her son as a token of thanks for the lifts given to her on numerous occasions by Gil, no trouble at all to him as he passed her house on the way home, but appreciated by the old lady when weighed down by her diligently gathered harvest from field and hedgerow.

We knew from experience their potency, especially that made from her elderberry flowers, palest gold and transparent as a topaz.

Deceived by the innocence of its smooth sweetness into drinking the best part of a bottle between us, we remember vividly the delayed effect of a well aimed sledge hammer and the resulting headache.

Willing to risk another, we sat after supper sampling the rich black currant wine and roasting chestnuts at the blazing fire which, with the departure of the wind from the north was behaving itself impeccably, and we had been able to sit unsmoked and unchoked for several days.

We sat revelling in the warmth and peace, the lamp light casting it's gentle rays on the glistening tree and the fireplace beam, hung with its garland of holly and ribbons.

"Aren't we lucky? We're sitting right in the middle of our own Christmas card. The only thing that's missing is Father Christmas coming down the chimney."

"I wouldn't advise him to try it just yet," Gil answered drily. "Unless he's got enough snow on his boots to put out the fire. He could do himself a mischief."

Turning on the wireless, we listened to the pure, soaring notes of the Kings College choir singing carols. Gloria in Excelsis! We sang with such heartiness that Tack's ears twitched in protest and Maud sprang off my lap to join him on the rug.

Just before midnight Gil went out to stoke up, and called to me to come and listen. Frost sparkled like icing sugar on the garden in the light from the door, and the sky was black velvet, star studded. The sound of the Minster bells came clearly to us in the stillness, ringing out their message of joy. No other sound penetrated the darkness until we heard heavy footsteps coming towards us up the lane, breaking the spell. The clash of steel tipped boots hit the hard surface of the road, and a deep voice called out "Goodnight! Merry Christmas!" as Bob Chatham continued his unsteady way home and his dog gave an answering bark of welcome.

As the footsteps died away, the silence was absolute. "The bells have stopped." I said. "It's Christmas Day."

Gil put an arm round me as we ducked in through the doorway, saying "It's cold. Let's go to bed," and kissed me under the mistletoe.

Chapter 14

We came to the conclusion that Maud was courting. For days she had been disappearing for long stretches at a time, sometimes staying out all night despite the severe weather, returning in the morning disheveled and ravenously hungry. It was not until sounds of discord, savage and shrill, reached us from various parts of the garden that we realised that we had been infiltrated by cats from all corners of Dorset, who were measuring up to one another noisily and spitefully in a bid for Maud's hand. We behaved like fussing parents, picking out the suitor we considered to be the most eligible, and dismissing the less desirable element, until we finally narrowed the field to two - an all white, handsome and debonair, with an obviously impeccable pedigree, and a local cat we knew by sight, a large battle scarred tabby with a slight nervous shake of the head, whose pleasant personality made up for his lack of physical attributes - while Maud behaved in the most disgracefully flirtatious way, conducting her amorous affairs on the doorstep with total disregard for decorum. Very soon, to our relief, the suitors melted away, the air was no longer rent with screeching argument, and Maud was content to return once more to full bed and board, which was as well, the weather having worsened, and the likelihood of sleet announced on the wireless.

One morning we woke to find a layer of ice on the water in our bedside tumblers, and in the dim morning light from the window saw icicles hanging from the thatch, tiny stalactites like irregular teeth, reminding me as I lay drowsy and fanciful, postponing the moment before throwing off the blankets, of the wicked Tooth Goblins in the Gibbs Dentifrice advertisements of childhood, who attacked the Good Tooth Fairies in their ivory castle if we children neglected to clean our teeth.

Going down to fill the water buckets, we found the well frozen, so that we had to prime it with kettles of boiling water before the pump handles would budge an inch. The landscape was still, a spell cast on it by a fine dusting of frost, softening the outline of the bare trees and turning them pale and ghostly against the leaden sky.

Maud, serene and home loving again, sensibly spent most of her days curled up in an empty seed box in the propagating house, catlike, making the most of a bad situation, a graceful paw wrapped round her nose and the soft fur scarcely rising and falling as she breathed. We happily joined her there, as the time had come to transfer the young plants into the small heated house, which had been sterilised and double dug, a back breaking job, with a base dressing of bone meal, hoof and horn and potash, among other ingredients, as recommended by the Horticultural Advisory Service, who always helpful, had taken a sample of our soil for analysis.

Only too aware of our responsibility for our first crop from seed to full maturity, we were grateful for any information which could be gleaned from books or from asking questions of fellow nurserymen, who with very few exceptions were happy to give us the benefit of their long experience. Ernie Brown was one such, a large ruddy faced man who, in addition to tomatoes, grew the most magnificent exhibition chrysanthemums, and it was always a pleasure to drive up to the nursery and see acre upon acre of breathtaking colour. The Queen of the Autumn he called them, and we determined that one day we would grow them. In later years our ambition was realised, but because of our lack of ground space, ours were a different variety, in pots grown under glass, a sea of pinks and yellows and bronze to be boxed and marketed throughout the year.

Now that we had emptied the propagating house of all but Maud, we were able to sew the seeds for the cold house crop. We chose Moneymaker for its consistent sweetness and uniformity of shape and size and sowed them thickly in trays. Three weeks later they were ready to be pricked out, using an ingenious template left to us by our predecessors made of board, from which protruded twenty four short pieces of cane. Pressed into each tray of compost, it produced the necessary holes into which the tiny plants were placed.

Tack took no interest in this exercise, as there was no digging going on and offered no excitement. Instead he bustled about the garden, his thick winter coat protecting him from the cold, and suffering only the frustration of not being able to dig up his bones. He liked to bring to light a different bone each day, remembering exactly where each was buried and taking them in rotation as if they were numbered on a map carried in his brain. Each was examined and appraised for its ripeness and succulence, sniffed and gnawed, and if it was considered still gastronomically interesting, returned to its place. He was put out by the difficulty of digging the hard ground, which took so much longer and used a great deal more energy, and watching him at work, puffing with exertions, his front legs moving at great speed like piston rods, we used to say that were he a human, his face would be bright red.

The day's work done, we noticed as we hurried up to the cottage, the icy air cutting through our clothes, that Farmer Parsons had taken in his herd to winter quarters, and we missed the companionable moving pattern of black and white beyond the hedge. Hungry gulls had flown inland to take their place, swooping down in vociferous numbers to strut and squabble and snatch up what food there was to be found in the frozen mud of the trampled field.

It was during this cold spell that Freddie brought his new wife to see us, complaining bitterly of the inhospitality of our climate. His marriage came as a shock to us, and to those who knew him in the R.A.F. as a dedicated bachelor. In middle age, while holidaying in Spain, he had fallen irrevocably in love with a widowed lady, and was now retired and sharing her villa in Malaga, a youth again despite the greying hair, to whom something unforeseen and wonderful had happened. As he explained to Gil, who always said of Freddie that he had a girl for every day of the week and one in reserve, "The moment I met her it was chocks away, old boy."

Liz, the object of his devotion and wonderment, was tall, cool and model thin, her blonde hair faultless and beautiful in a French pleat, her nails shell pink talons and half a hundredweight of charm bracelets jingled as she talked. She and Freddie were in England on pressing family business, otherwise nothing would have prised them from Spanish shores, and they found it so cold in the cottage that they sat in their overcoats and scarves, their deeply tanned faces looking remarkably robust in contrast to our pinched paleness. They sat

71

holding hands, loving glances passing between them, and Liz murmuring asides in Spanish which I found disconcerting, unable to decide whether they were endearments or comments best not understood by their host and hostess.

Anxious to move on to somewhere warmer, and who could blame them, they took us to dinner in Sandbanks, Gil looking unfamiliar, having exchanged his sweater and jacket for a dark suit and collar and tie. Our lack of any social activity since coming to the Homestead, while enjoyed by us both, had made us lazy, and the temptation to go about in "slop order" as Gil called it was strong. There was no way I was going to match the vision of loveliness in our sitting room had I worked at it for a week, but I made an effort to produce an acceptable image. Chilly nylons replaced my faded cords, and high heeled shoes encased my feet which were more accustomed to gumboots and thick socks.

We had a lovely evening, and were magnificently wined and dined in warmth and elegance, overlooking the harbour, a fringe of lights casting a thousand reflections in the dark water.

Discussing the evening as, teeth chattering, we scrambled into bed, and planning to accept Liz's invitation to stay with them when cash and commitments permitted, I said I thought it might be rather nice to feel warm more often. "How do you fancy a villa in Spain?"

"All that blue sky. So boring," came from under the bedclothes.

I prattled on, stimulated by the wine and gaiety of the occasion, and was soon aware of a gentle snoring which told me that I had lost my audience. Turning out the lamp and pulling the blankets up over my ears I said "Oh well. Perhaps I'll just settle for a thatched ice box in Dorset."

The wind was still bitter, cutting through our clothes as we hurried down to the glasshouses the next morning, and it was a joy to open the door of the heated house to be greeted by a blast of warm air and the musty smell of humid compost. Despite the bleakness, a few brave snowdrops had already pushed up through the frozen lawn to form a ring of small clumps round the apple tree. The birds were quarrelsome, and we could never understand their lack of common sense in wasting their precious energy fighting over one morsel of food when there was plenty for all.

One particularly cold day Gil hurried shivering into the cottage, taking off his woollen mittens and rubbing his hands together.

"Not much of a fire for your sovereign."

Not much of a fire for anyone, since the change in the wind had started it sulking and belching again, and the chimney was drawing lazily and fitfully. Gil's criticism had become a stock saying, and was based on an incident which took place during the war at the R.A.F. Station at St. Athans in South Wales.

An inspection by King George VI had been arranged, and a posse of high ranking officers assembled at the main gate to greet their Monarch. Due to a misunderstanding, the royal party arrived at the wrong gate at the other end of the camp, to find no reception committee, and it was decided that the King should be driven straight to the Officers' Mess, where the Mess Steward had just lit a fire in the ante room. It was a bitterly cold day, and the fire like ours was no respecter of persons and in a sulky mood, smouldering inhospitably.

Soon afterwards, the Station Commander, having been warned of the situation, arrived in a state of confusion accompanied by the top brass. He found His Majesty standing with his back to the fireplace, hands behind his back, and instead of the expected right royal reprimand was greeted with the words "Not much of a fire for your Sovereign."

That evening we spent hours wrapped in our blankets, coughing and cursing, having decided that the budget would not run to a visit to Jethro's blazing fire. Even the old black stove, which we had spurned and thrown out, could not have behaved like this, and we vowed that before another winter the dog grate would follow it out through the door, and the chimney thoroughly investigated.

Nothing for it, we decided, but to damp down the smouldering embers, wrap Tack up in his basked, place Maud's blanket on her chair, and wend our way to bed clutching our hot water bottles. The wind took the door and blew it back in a strong gust as Gil put on his jacket and he and Tack went out for a last look at things. Seconds later there was a thunderous banging on the door. Only Tom Butler had ever called as late as this, and even he, I reasoned, would not venture out on such a night, however strong his compulsion to entertain us. Opening it a few inches, preparing to tell him sternly to go home, I was blinded by the light of a powerful flash lamp, which when lowered revealed a large policeman in a dark cape and helmet. Stooping down to the level of the low lintel he asked if he might come in. As he stood there, his heavy cape billowing out from his sides in the howling wind, he seemed like a sinister black bat in the darkness, and a sense of foreboding gripped me as I stepped aside to allow him in. Without his helmet he still found it necessary to stoop to avoid the beams, and seemed to fill the small room, as my worst imaginings were confirmed, he told me that my father was dead. Earlier that evening he had suffered a heart attack, and as we had no telephone my mother had requested the help of the local constabulary, a member of which now stood before me, the reluctant bearer of sad news.

We had known for some months that my father's illness was grave, and my mother had cared for him through a long period of great strain, but when it came I was unprepared for what I knew must come. He had visited us only once in late autumn, having expressed a wish to see "what we were up to" as he put it, but the day had been overcast and chilly, and the occasion marred by our anxiety that we would be unable to keep him as warm as his frailty required, and we promised that we would bring him again in the spring. Now he would not see the thick bands of daffodils circling the apple tree, and the lapwing strutting in the fields, their backs gleaming like jewels in the April sun or enjoy the scent of the honeysuckle which filled the garden with its sweetness.

Chapter 15

March blustered in with winds strong but kinder, not so much a lion as a boisterous puppy, chasing the white puffy clouds across a clear sky and teasing the catkin tails in a merry dance. The birds still waited hungrily in the laurel for titbits, but we thought we detected a certain jauntiness in the robin's song, and noticed several blue tits inspecting the nesting box on the garage wall. Yellow and purple crocus stood alongside the snowdrops, and in keeping with the general burgeoning of flora and fauna all around us, Maud's spreading waistline told us that we were expecting a happy event.

We decided it would be safe, now that the wind had moved into a warmer quarter, to move the sweet peas from their perch up high in the cold house out into the trenches which Gil had triple dug on the south side of the small house. It has been said of sweet peas that they have a delicate growth, very deep rooting, the smell of an angel and the appetite of a crocodile. We bought pounds of offal from the local abattoir, a sickening place smelling of blood and fear, to line the bottom of the trenches before putting in the young plants and placing cloches over them to protect them until April.

If we needed further evidence of the promise of spring, Mr. Potts and his hat had emerged from hibernation. The familiar grumbling reached us as we worked, and to our delight it was no longer a monologue. Mrs. Potts was answering back. Perhaps the long winter confinement had driven her to rebel, but whatever the reason small querulous sounds drifted over the hedge, and we knew that at last the worm had turned.

Before we became fully occupied with the planting out in the cold houses later in the month, we thought it would be a good idea to tackle a domestic improvement. We missed our books, which were still packed in cases in the store room, and as the unevenness of walls and floor made a built-in bookcase an impossibility, the only place to use was the recess in which stood the zinc copper, above a small grate, with a hole knocked into the side of the chimney breast to enable the smoke to escape.

The copper was heavy but quite easily dislodged, and as I helped Gil to ease it out I leapt back as a large spider ambled out into the room. I say ambled because it certainly was not running, and seemed disoriented by this violation of its privacy behind the copper. A frowsy, slummocky spider, clearly put out and not quite sure where it was going. I knew exactly where it was going, and as my chair was only a foot away from the recess I was thankful it had waited until now to make its entrance, when Gil was at hand to throw it into the garden.

Mercifully, we had been almost entirely free of creepy crawlies during the winter months, and of mice thanks to Maud, although a week or two before she had presented us with a live toad, which resented it, and proved very difficult to catch. Each time we stretched out a hand it croaked loudly and leapt away, until after may attempts to capture it we had the idea of dropping a shoe box over it to quieten it and curtail its progress. We though we had been clever, but the toad thought otherwise and refused to stay still or silent, voicing his anger even more stridently. The sight of a box hopping round the room was fascinating to Tack and reduced us to helpless laughter. Finally Gil managed to hold it down long enough for me to slip a piece of card between it and the floor, and he was then able to lift the whole thing up and release the indignant creature, still objecting throatily, into the garden.

Having removed the copper there was some repair work to be done to the cob walls of the surrounding area, which Gil with his newly acquired expertise, rendered and whitewashed. We found it would take three deep shelves which rested on battens screwed into the sides, leaving enough space underneath to take the coal scuttle or log basket, and when filled with some of our smaller books made a pleasing extension to the fireplace.

Sitting beside it a few evenings later, my cup of tea on the shelf and feeling smugly certain that we were free of unwelcome visitors, I was horrified to see the saucer covered in black ants all happily dining off my biscuit. The spider was not the only one to be disturbed and there must have been a nest in the brickwork, but search as we might we could not discover the source and they continued to invite themselves to tea in increasing numbers.

We have a profound respect for ants and feel they could teach us all a lesson in industry. To prove how little justice there is in this world, they were frequently set upon by their larger cousins, the red ants, of which there were a great many on the nursery, orange in colour rather then red and deadly, which Gil later discovered to his cost, and we often witnessed brief skirmishes in which the red ants, larger and more savage, stung their smaller opponents to death. Whereupon, and this fascinated us, survivors would rush out and under the noses of the enemy go to great lengths to recover their dead and carry them home. This was obviously important to them, and we watched them heaving and pulling at the little corpses, trying again and again to stagger away, holding them in front of them like babies.

Obsessive about ensuring the survival of the species after so many battle casualties, there was always a panic stricken two-way traffic of egg carriers. This, it seemed to us, was where their efficiency broke down, and one wondered which were coming and which going, and whether they themselves knew. Presumably they did, and just watching their frantic activity was quite exhausting, and we would have liked to help by picking each one up, egg and all, between our fingers, and depositing it at its destination, but as we were not too certain where they wanted to go, we left well alone.

Chapter 16

The young plants looked sturdy in their pots as we started carrying them into the cold houses for planting out. There were just over twelve hundred in all, half of which we had bought from Ernie, as we had not sufficient space to produce all we would need to fill the two houses, and a few dozen or so we kept for customers' orders.

We planted along string guide lines, six rows to a house, a hundred to a row a foot apart, using a heavy metal dibber to make the holes, and dropped a pot into each. The pale sun of the past few days had already begun to warm the soil, and with all ventilators open we found our sweaters too hot to wear. Cheeky Chappie flew in to lend us moral support, in a state of excitement and hoping for a few hand-outs. "You'll have to find your own worms, chum," Gil said discouragingly, coming in with another batch of pots. "Haven't got time today." Once every hole was filled we tapped out each plant, replaced it in the hole and firmed it in, watering well. It was good to see the houses full once more, and we were determined that this crop would be every bit as good as the last.

Going up to the cottage for tea, pleased with our day's work and in a silly mood, fooling about and indulging in horseplay, which had we been children would have prompted my mother to say that it would all end in tears before bedtime. It almost did one day before we were married, when Gil's fist accidentally connected with my eye. He was devastated when after a few seconds it was a magnificent sight, black and blue and quite closed. That evening we had planned to make a trip to the cinema in Salisbury to see "Scott of the Antarctic" and not wanting to make too much of the incident I said we would still go and I would be fine. It was as much as I could do to sit through the film, peering out of one eye at the endless white landscape, and by the time the gallant Captain Oates staggered out into the night saying the immortal words "I'm just going outside. I may be gone for some time," I was ready to go with him.

Gil invariably won these childish battles, but Tack always weighed in on my side with wild enjoyment, and between us we managed to give him a pretty hard time. On this occasion, deciding that he could take no more, he collapsed on the sofa saying "Two against one. Not fair. Pax!! I collapsed beside him, and still laughing we became aware that we were not alone. At the open door stood a pallid gentleman in a clerical collar, a look of astonished disgust on his face as if he had just caught us out in an act of gross indecency. We both leapt to our feet, Gil holding out his hand and saying "Good afternoon, Padre. come in."

"Yes," I said brightly and tactlessly, "Do come in. Take a pew," thinking how nice it was of him to call and welcome us to his parish. It became plain that he was not here to enquire into the spiritual needs of his flock, but merely to purchase tomato plants for his greenhouse. We watched as stiff backed he bore the box of plants to his car, giving us not so much a smile as a small rearrangement of his face, and realised as it slid smoothly away that not only was it a Rolls Royce, but chauffeur driven, and it struck us as an unlikely indulgence for the vicar of a small rural parish.

"Well, well," chuckled Gil. "No wonder he's no time for the peasants."

It looked to us as if the birth of Maud's kittens was imminent. She was ravenous, eating for an unknown quantity and demanding snacks at all hours of the day. She wandered away very little, staying within the garden, and spent most of her time asleep on the camp bed. We discussed what was to be done with the litter, and decided we would allow her to keep one, and find homes for the remainder, when weaned. Each time our cats presented us with kittens that was what we always intended, but over the years we found that placing kittens with responsible people was far from easy, and always there seemed to be one which no one wanted or which was too charming to part with, which is why we eventually found ourselves sharing our home with six, one magnificent male and five females, all of whom in the course of time were neutered and lived to old age, greatly loved, and when their time came, deeply mourned.

It is one thing sharing one's home with chosen friends, but quite another playing unwilling host to a swarm of ants. The bookshelves were never free of them, even when deprived of their biscuit snacks, and when each time we took a book from the shelf they ran out from the pages we knew we would have to act, and sprinkled ant powder on every surface. It had no effect at all, and they continued to scurry to and from, mercifully having left their eggs at home.

Quite by chance I read an article in a woman's magazine about a young couple who had bought a large ancient house in a poor state of repair, and found themselves infested with mice which, having had the place to themselves for years, refused to vacate, despite all possible persuasion.

Their plight came to the notice of Lady Dowding, and I hope my memory is correct here, who had written books on the subject of communication between humans and all other forms of animal life, convinced that one species can make itself understood by another, and maintaining that plagues and infestations could be dispelled by the simple expedient of appealing to them to leave, a service she had successfully given on countless occasions. The couple took up her offer of help as a last resort, not hopeful of any positive result, and were astonished, therefore, when after Lady Dowding had visited the house and asked the persistent guests to leave, within a few days there was peace.

I was intrigued by this story, and decided that as no special powers seemed to be required, I would put it to the test. I waited until Gil had gone out, sat down in my chair, and feeling foolish and self-conscious, addressed the bookshelves, telling our guests how much I admired them and that they were welcome to share my biscuits, but they had become an inconvenience and would they kindly leave and run all over someone else's books. I said nothing to Gil until the following evening, when I noticed the number was greatly reduced. Within a few days there was barely an ant to be seen, and they never returned.

I have never been able to explain it, and would have been glad of the opportunity to try it out on the army of mice which had invaded the cottage in the summer.

One thing I am sure of. It would never have worked with spiders. There has to be an empathy, which is something I could not achieve, and the thought of being close enough to address them personally is something I would rather not contemplate.

Chapter 17

We heard the cuckoo in the early evening as we walked with Tack to the spinney. A few seconds later it was answered by another from somewhere up by the main road, and we knew that spring had come again. The earth had slept and now had woken refreshed, to scatter the hedgerows with wild violets and touch the countryside with fresh green life, and as we came up the farm track for home, the beech trees had turned to gold and the glasshouses to flame in the sinking sun.

I remarked that Maud had not been seen since breakfast, which in view of her prodigious appetite of late, was cause for speculation. We had no way of knowing whether, like many domestic cats, she would seek the company of humans for the birth, or whether she would revert to the wild and go off into the fields to find a private place where she could be alone. I hoped she would stay with us, and in anticipation of the event had replaced her box with a larger, shallower one, comfortably lined with clean blanket, and with one side cut away.

There was no sign of her when we returned, so the store room seemed the obvious first place to look. We had no need to search further. She was lying in the box suckling five snow white kittens, and looking immensely pleased with herself.

"How lovely! She's had them at home," I said, kneeling down to stroke her. "You are a clever girl, Maud. They're beautiful." Something she already knew. In truth they resembled five large, blind mice, but then all babies are beautiful to their mothers.

We took her some food and left her in peace, jamming the door open just enough to allow her to squeeze in and out, and placing a heavy weight behind it so that Tack would be unable to blunder in and provoke her into defending her family resulting in, at the very least, a scratched nose.

From their colour we thought we had no difficulty in identifying their father, but the following day it seemed a little strange to see the amiable tabby sitting in the middle of the lawn, as if instinctively he had known of the birth and had come to acknowledge his progeny.

The following afternoon we went out in the van for a short time, and for some reason which escapes me we did not take Tack and left him in the garden, with the instruction to stay. We had left him many times before, and knew that he would not venture beyond the white chain which divided the driveway from the lane. We drove in expecting to see him in his usual place, on guard and alert for intruders. No welcoming bark reached us as we walked up the path, and then a hideous sight met our eyes. Small mangled bodies lay on the lawn, tufts of white fur scattered over the grass, and as we stared in horror, Tack emerged from the open door of the store room with the last lifeless kitten in his mouth. Maud had thought it safe to leave her litter to stretch her legs for a short while, which Tack must have noted before pushing his way through the gap and embarking on his grisly massacre. Gil, white faced with fury, grabbed him by the scruff of the neck and beat him with his open hand before shutting him in the cottage while we cleared up the gruesome remains.

Perhaps jealousy had gripped Tack because of the attention we were paying to Maud, or perhaps in Maud's absence, the kittens had mewed and thinking they were rats and easily accessible had looked on them as easy sport. We would never know, but I wept for Maud and resolved that she should have at least one kitten to feed. I rode off on my bicycle round Wimborne, calling first at the farm up on the main road, hoping that one of their many farm cats might have a spare kitten no older than a day or two. I phoned the R.S.P.C.A., who were sympathetic but unable to help at that time, and continued on my way, calling at random at houses and shops. I eventually found one, a little tabby scrap of a thing, not too robust, but as it was one of a large litter the owner was thankful to part with it, and tucking it warmly inside my jacket I cycled the short distance home to find Maud searching and calling, distressed at her loss, and put the tiny kitten in the box.

I should have known that an animal will seldom accept another's young unless the scent of her own is upon it. Sadly, Maud would have nothing to do with it, refusing to feed it, and to my dismay finally pushed it out of the box, where it died.

We were both consumed with guilt, Gil because he had allowed rage to overcome reason, and had punished Tack for doing what we had many times incited him to do, and for which until now he had shown little aptitude. Either of us could have made sure the store room door was shut before leaving, and had we done so Maud would still have her family and the hapless little substitute would have been alive. All we could do now was to give her, on a practical level, anti-lactation pills, and a great deal of love.

Chapter 18

The plants were progressing well, and were now between twelve and fourteen inches high and in need of support, so our next job was to string them on fillis suspended from wires in the roof. Most of them had flowered, and they looked to us sturdy and healthy, and we tried to visualise the crop as we hoped it was going to look, heavy with beautiful trusses and promising a bumper yield. In the heated house the plants were already showing signs of ripening, and we thought it would not be too long before our first pick of the year.

Having spent the day stringing, we decided we had earned a day out, and I leapt at Gil's suggestion that we pay a visit to my mother whom we had not seen more than a few times since my father's death, and knew how much she welcomed visitors.

The following Sunday, on a typical April morning, we drove through Wareham and turned off the main road for Lulworth, sun and showers in equal measure combining to enhance the sight and smell of the hedgerows and early blossom. The familiar red flag was flying from a pole as we reached the ranges, to indicate that firing was in progress, the moorland on either side of us deeply scarred with hideous ruts from constant tank activity.

We came level with the gates of Lulworth Castle, clumps of primroses scattering the grass verge under the high walls, when there was an ominous sound which could only mean one thing. We had a flat tyre.

"Just our luck." Gil got out of the van removing his jacket. "We'll have to get it mended when we get there." In no time the tyre was replaced and we drove down the steep hill past the barracks into the village. Today, in high summer, cars and coachloads of holidaymakers and sightseers descend upon it in thousands and there is no peace, but on that day the village was at its Sunday best and only the sound of the church bell announcing that morning service was about to begin broke the silence. Not unexpectedly, the vicar was the only one in business, and the garage was shut, but as our van was new we were confident that we would make the journey home without trouble.

We left for home late in the evening, having spent a happy day, walking round the cove in the afternoon, and breathing in the strong air as we sat on the group of rocks where a fresh water spring bubbles up through the pebbles. The waves breaking against the base of the cliffs at the mouth of the cove sent up showers of sparkling foam, and the sun was warm on our faces.

Coming out onto the main Wareham Road there was suddenly a sound like a pistol shot from the near side, and the telltale clunk, clunk, clunk told us the worst - that we had another puncture.

"BLAST!" Gil brought his fist down on the steering wheel. "That's what's known as sod's law. What do we do now?"

We sat fuming and trying to decide the best course of action. We knew there would be no garage open in Wareham, and there was no telephone box for miles. We considered settling down for the night in the van, but as we had no covering of any kind and the evening had already become quite chilly, we were certain that if we slept at all, by daylight we should be stiff and cold as frogs. We came to the conclusion that there was nothing for it but to walk the seven miles back to Lulworth.

Tack seemed the only one delighted at the prospect, and romped along ahead of us. The rain had brought out the strong scent of gorse but Tack was not interested in flora when the smell of fauna was titillating his nostrils, and he yelped with excitement at the prospect of putting up a rabbit or two.

We knew the road well, having travelled it countless times by car, but this was a different road, a stranger to us in the moonlight, which threw the branches of shrubs into stark relief against the sky, the miles of flat moorland on either side ghostly in the bright whiteness.

At regular intervals along the route were large signs a foot or more back from the road warning of DANGER - UNEXPLODED SHELLS, so that we had to keep Tack within bounds each time his enthusiasm got the better of him for fear he might take off across the open land and disturb, not a rabbit, but something far more sinister.

I looked nervously round. "I hope the army doesn't decide it could do with some moving target practice."

I had made it my business to treat tanks with great respect after a hair raising experience with a convoy at the beginning of the war. My father had been posted to Larkhill, near Salisbury Plain, and my elder sister and I were working on a local farm for eightpence halfpenny an hour. Not a princely wage packet at the end of the week, but it was a ritual on Friday nights after a day cutting kale, muck spreading, threshing or whatever the current requirement was, to walk down to the small village shop in Shrewton and blew the lot on cosmetics and cigarettes, with the occasional bottle of Optrex to remove the straw from our bloodshot eyes.

Striding down the hill in the fading light we heard a rumbling behind us which grew to a terrifying roar as a line of lurching tanks bore down on us, unaware that we were in their path. They travelled without lights, and we had no torch to flash in the hope that it might make them aware of us. There was no question of standing aside as they passed as the road was too narrow and was flanked on both sides by steep banks.

Panic stricken, we stood and waved our arms in a futile gesture, shouting at the top of our lungs, and realising with horror that they were not going to stop and were coming relentlessly on, we flung ourselves flat against the bank, hanging desperately on to tufts of grass, slippery after rain, to prevent ourselves from sliding down to be crushed by the caterpillar tracks so terrifyingly close to our rubber booted legs.

I comforted myself that should anything come lurching over the moorlands towards us this time, there was plenty of room for escape, but I need not have worried. Not a sound of military activity reached us, and the eerie stillness was broken only by the occasional hoot of an owl and our footsteps on the wet road as we came level with the old prisoner of war camp with its dilapidated huts, empty now of all but the ghosts of German men who had spent their remaining war years behind barbed wire in an enemy country. Many of them had been released during the day to work on nearby farms, and after the cessation of hostilities a number had forsaken their Fatherland for the Dorset countryside, and married local girls, in time becoming respected members of the community.

Farther up the lane on the opposite side was another familiar landmark which we called our little house. It stood, alone and long deserted, ivy growing through the mullioned windows which had many years before been shattered by the constantly firing guns, and as we passed the fallen fence and peered into the once pretty garden, now an overgrown jungle of bramble, we wondered about it's former occupants and thought how sad we should have been to leave our cottage to fall into neglect and eventual destruction.

We though Tack's short legs would surely tire and had visions of having to carry him on the last lap, but he showed no signs of weariness. I would have been glad of a piggy-back as my shoes were not designed for marathons and a blister had begun to form on my heel. I covered the last mile in my stockinged feet, and as Bindon came into sight, bathed in moonlight, we arrived at my startled mother's door, and fell into bed, needing no rocking to sleep that night.

Chapter 19

The following morning, as soon as we could get our two tyres mended, we set off for home, and heading down the lane we were startled to see standing at the gate a spanking vintage Bentley, its gleaming dark green bonnet, held by a heavy leather strap, looking as long as the cottage was deep. Gil leapt out of the van saying "I know that car!" and as he spoke a tall good looking man with close cropped hair walked down the path towards us.

"Dickie!" Gil rushed up to him, grinning broadly and pumped his hand up and down as if he were filling buckets at the well. I was introduced to this warmly smiling man, who it transpired had been Gil's friend at the R.A.F. Station, Hucknall after the war, and was currently a Flight Engineer engaged on testing the Princess Flying Boats at Cowes.

He stayed to have coffee with us, during which he and Gil caught up on news of mutual acquaintances and swapped reminiscences, and after a conducted tour of the nursery, he drove away with a throaty roar and a promise to come and see us again soon. In fact it was to be two years before his second visit, and this time he came not in the Bentley but in the Princess. One day we head a deep throbbing which as it came nearer increased to an almighty roar, and we raced outside to see the gigantic flying boat, its wingspan five times the length of the cottage, thunder over us at a height of about five hundred feet. We gazed upward, waving wildly, rooted to the spot by the sight of this monstrous white bird, and deafened by sound.

We breathed a sigh of relief to see the thatch had not been sucked into the slipstream, but the sparrows nesting in the east end had a nasty turn, and we swear we saw the cottage tremble.

Having assured himself that our night away had not harmed the crop, although the temperature in the heated house had dropped appreciably, Gil decided that the outside temperature was sufficiently high to warrant the removal of the cloches from the sweet peas, which meant that they would need to be strung individually on fillis supported by a wooden structure eight feet high. Once they reached the top they would be untied and laid along the ground so that the "cut and come again plants" as they were known, could bloom a second time. Our outlay on good quality seed proved to be a good investment, and the result was a superb crop of long stemmed blooms of infinite colour variety.

Tidying up the garden, I reflected that keen gardeners do not like daisies on their lawns, and the sight of just one of these perky little heads in the grass is enough to give them apoplexy. I am not a keen gardener, therefore I find daisies growing on my lawn a delightful sight and a perfect excuse for not mowing it. Maud kept me company while I tried to quell the exuberant new spring growth of weeds, having greeted us on our return plaintively demanding to know where we had been and what happened to breakfast? We were happy to see that she seemed to have completely recovered from the trauma of losing her family, and was herself behaving like a kitten, streaking like a rocket up the apple tree, frightening off the blackbird who flew to the garage roof uttering his pit-pit-pit of alarm, and having had her fun peering mischievously through the tight pink budded branches.

The musty tang of the flowering currant mingled with the sweet scent of honeysuckle and wallflowers, and a brisk breeze was teasing the pollen from the hazel catkins, which usually meant that Gil would be sneezing by the time he reached the drive. I was cutting some daffodils for the cottage when I heard a shout from the direction of the glasshouses. A second later I was startled to see Gil streaking past me up the path, tearing off his trousers as he ran into the cottage, and I knew that it was not hay fever that was the problem.

"Quick!" he yelled. "I'm being eaten alive!"

I dropped the daffodils and raced in after him to find that he had taken off the rest of his clothes and was frantically flicking red ants off himself. Dozens of the insects swarmed over the lower part of his body and angry red patches were appearing in many places. Anyone who has ever been stung by a red ant will know how painful it can be. He refused to keep still and broke into a frenzied war dance while I followed him round the kitchen brushing off the wretched creatures and stamping on them as they fell to the floor.

As the last ones perished and Gil realised that he was not in danger of being eaten to the bone, but was just stung in one or two unfortunate places, his colour returned to normal and he slowed down to a kind of soft shoe shuffle. I suddenly could not control myself and began to laugh. For a moment Gil looked outraged at my lack of sympathy and unseemly mirth, then he too began to see the funny side and threw back his head in a great bellow of laughter, until we were both sitting on the mat giggling feebly while I dabbed him with anti-histamine lotion.

I made him a cup of strong sweet tea while he put on fresh clothes, and I noticed that his trousers were firmly tucked into long socks inside his boots as he went back down the path declaring total war on every red ant on the nursery.

Later, looking more cheerful, he came into the kitchen giving a passable imitation of a fanfare of trumpets, holding in his outstretched hand a solitary tomato. I could see this was not just any old tomato. This was the first of our very first crop grown from seed, and a perfect specimen. This required a solemn tasting, and as I cut it into meticulous halves I said "There really ought to be ceremony."

"Well," Gil laughed, "I'll just pop down to the cellar and bring up the Bollinger."

In the absence of champagne we settled for tea, and raised our mugs for the toast.

"To the crop."

"To the crop" I echoed. "God bless it."

Chapter 20

There was plenty of work to be done in the glasshouses, and as we scuttled down the path it was raining steadily. The smell of wallflowers was strong and delicious, and the macracarpa bushes stood festooned in glistening webs. April wept her golden tears on the widespread branches of Pok Pok's tree, showering us with creamy white blossom as we passed, and beating an erratic rataplan on the rusty oil drum lying in the long grass beneath.

Tack had looked at the weather and decided not to accompany us, going back to his basket to await an improvement. Maud, similarly, had opened one eye and prepared to sleep all day in the manner of cats when there is nothing more exciting on the agenda.

"It's alright for some," said Gil as we ran through the door into the moist, warm atmosphere. Pinching out the small side shoots to maintain a sturdy growth in the main stem was a satisfying and relaxing job, and there was scarcely a sound as we moved steadily down the rows except for the rain running in rivulets down the glass.

Later that day, as I came down the path with mugs of tea, the sound of a dog barking came clearly across the fields in the damp air. "That dog's still barking," I said. "Can you hear it? I've heard it on and off all day. I wonder where it is."

"Probably tied up somewhere," Gil said absently, concentrating on the job in hand.

As our day's work came to an end I began to look forward to my bath. On Friday nights, after supper, we walked down the lane clutching our wash bags and towels to Pat and Millie Haines, where a warm welcome awaited us. Pat was a short, rotund man with immense shoulders and a slow, gentle way of talking, and a fondness for whiskey after his day's toil. Millie was his opposite in every way, tall and beanstalk thin with a sharp way of speaking, and was never without a cigarette which hung from the middle of her mouth as she spoke. It was hard to concentrate on what she was saying, as the cigarette jigged up and down with the movement of her lips, and the mind was concentrated on the inch or so of ash which hung precariously from its end, and one waited to see how long it would remain there before falling unnoticed onto her pinafore front.

For one night in the week I was one of the languorous ladies in the magazines, lying luxuriously in hot, scented water to my chin, the only drawback being that Millie always cleaned the bath with paraffin, and not only did the smell compete badly with the bath salts, but it made the bath slippery to a lethal degree, making it so that without care one could turn turtle and sink without trace. But that was an ungrateful criticism, especially as, all ablutions completed, there was always a large glass of sherry waiting for us to set the seal on the occasion.

The sound of the dog barking woke me in the night, the deep bark followed now by a long drawn out howl. A miserable sound which Gil also had heard. Still half asleep, he said "Tack's dreaming again," but although he occasionally howled in his sleep, we knew that this was not Tack but the dog we had heard all day. It continued through the night, until in desperation we closed the window and tried to sleep. But sleep would not come as we lay worrying about the dog and wondering whether it was caught in some sort of trap, and made up our minds that first thing in the morning we would try and find it, had not someone else already done so by then.

As soon as we had breakfasted, we started off over the fields, heading in the direction of the railway line, stopping every now and then to listen and confirm that we were going in the right direction. Tack was taking full advantage of an unexpectedly early walk, which after rain held great promise of a rabbit, or anything moving which was worth inspection and a possible chase. The steady downpour of the day before had brought out the strong sweet scent of the hawthorn in the hedgerows, the red buds and dark glossy leaves contrasting with the delicate pale green of the hazel.

Our Friesian friends were in the middle field, a pleasant sight as we had missed their company after they were moved into winter quarters. I called out to Mabel, who was identifiable by the large white circle on her side, and was quite the nosiest of the herd, taking a great interest in the activities at The Homestead, which she watched with untiring curiosity from her side of the hedge. This morning she was too busy enjoying the spring pasture to give us more than a fleeting glance before resuming her breakfast.

As we reached the railway line we could still hear the dog, but could see nothing to help us in our search. It still seemed to be some distance away and the sound was muffled by the tall embankment which stood alongside. We were convinced by now that we would find it somewhere up on the main road, but our way was blocked. The only thing for it was to return and continue our search by road.

After lunch we got in the van and took off down the lane determined to solve the mystery, and almost literally bumped into Monty Burgess who was coming in the opposite direction in his customary manner, much too fast and very erratically on the wrong side of the road.

We braked simultaneously and Monty shouted cheerfully that he was on his way to see us. He was the representative of a fertiliser firm and a frequent visitor to our part of Dorset, a man in his mid sixties and nearing retirement, and a charming figure immaculate in good country tweeds. We turned about and followed him back to the cottage, where over a cup of tea we related to him the story of the dog. He called himself a "cat man" and was the doting owner of two highly pedigreed and cosseted Siamese called Titti-Poo and Pitty-Sing, and was never without a ready supply of photographs of one or both to proudly show us. He had not made Maud's acquaintance until now, and was delighted that we now had what he called a "respectable family". Seeing her, as she came downstairs after her afternoon nap, he rushed to scoop her into his arms saying "OH! You little darling!" Maud would have none of it and showed her displeasure by spitting at him and wriggling indignantly out of his grasp. Monty smiled indulgently as she ran out of the door and stood on the path, her tail twitching angrily. We should have warned him that one did not take such liberties with Maud.

He was disturbed by our tale, and listened to the incessant barking. Eager to help us in our search and having no inclination for further calls that day, he said he would drive us up on to the main road and we would all look together. We took our lives in our hands as we shot down the lane and out onto the main road, Monty swerving from side to side and turning to look at Gil most of the time, which was an unnerving experience. Gil maintained that he only stayed alive due to the vigilance of the other drivers.

As we parked outside the small bakery which delivered our bread, the noise of the traffic and the swish of tyres on the wet road, coupled with a strong wind, made it very difficult to hear the barking, and we kept walking until the sound was quite clear. "It must be there!" I said excitedly as we neared a large house set well back from the road in an overgrown garden. We walked down the path, and knew that the barking, which became more feverish with the sound of our approach, came from a shed at the rear.

We went in search of the owner, a young man who walked towards us with a look of irritated enquiry on his face.

"Are you the owner of that dog?" asked Gil.

"Why do you want to know?"

"I'll tell you why I want to know. Because we can't sleep for his incessant barking, that's why. You've no right to keep a dog shut up like that."

"The poor thing," said Monty, looking reproachfully at the man and rubbing his hands together distractedly. "How could you?"

"He's alright. See for yourself," opening the door to reveal a large Alsation with amber eyes. "My brother didn't want him, so I've got him. He'll soon settle."

"Not shut up in there, he won't," snapped Gil. "If you can't give him a better deal than that I shall report you to the R.S.P.C.A."

"He'll settle. Don't you worry," patting the now silent dog on the head. "He's a nice dog. Just got to settle, that's all."

And settle it did. Soon we were sleeping undisturbed, happy in the knowledge that it was no longer shut in the shed and perhaps contentedly sharing the house with its new master.

Chapter 21

Mild panic set in when Dee's telegram arrived, asking if she could bring a friend down for the Whitsun weekend. Not that we were not delighted at the prospect of company, but it did present a few problems. Maurice was already booked in, which meant that the sleeping arrangements would require careful thought, and catering for five with the facilities at my disposal needed a certain amount of ingenuity on my part.

Dee's friend turned out to be Beth, a vivacious and easy mannered American girl who worked with her in London, and who from the moment of her arrival was determined to "muck in", insisting on trying her hand at watering the plants and filling buckets for domestic use with the same delight as she greeted the sight of the cottage, the first she had seen except on a picture postcard, and exclaiming at the low beams and undulating walls. "Quaint!" she said at regular intervals. It was all quaint. Even the privy, to which she was escorted by Tack who had fallen in love with her on sight, met with her excited approval.

"My! That's a kooky little john you have up there. I could see the cows out the window."

Maurice was at his most entertaining, and the girls, in a holiday mood and happy to be out of London for a day or two, were ready to laugh uproariously at his teasing. In fact, looking back on that weekend, laughter was the one ingredient which stands out in the memory, and it was one of those times when a group of people fits together, each one contributing eagerly to the relaxed and lighthearted atmosphere.

We decided the best way to sleep everyone was to give our bed to the girls, a sleeping bag on the let-down sofa to Maurice, and Gil and I would share the camp bed. Not a great success, this last, as the camp bed was barely more than two feet in width and the only way to stay on it was to lie on our sides, clamped together like sardines in a very small tin, neither daring to move. We might have made it through the night had it not been for the rug. Since our store of blankets was limited to say the least, we had pressed into service an old car rug, which turned out to be a mistake. It was a very hairy rug and the moment Gil drew it up over him he began to sneeze. A foot of space apiece if one keeps deathly still can just be tolerated. But regular violent eruptions make any hope of sleep an impossibility, and does nothing for the temper, and Gil finished up on the floor rolled in a blanket like a babe in swaddling clothes, while I selfishly and luxuriously stretched out over the whole two feet.

The sneezes grew less frequent, and were replaced by enthusiastic snores.

"Sshh!" I put out a hand to prod him into silence. "You're snoring. You'll wake everyone."

"How can I be snoring?" hissed Gil furiously. "I can't sleep."

In the morning our guests were insistent that they had heard nothing, Beth declaring that our strong Dorset air knocked her out cold, but I fancied they all looked a little hollow eyed.

Fried breakfasts were easily accomplished on the primus stoves, but I remember little of other meals except for salads with home grown tomatoes and shallots from the garden, and a beef casserole as large as the tin oven would hold.

"F.H.B." I muttered to Gil as he helped me in the kitchen. FAMILY HOLD BACK was a familiar warning in our family until my mother had satisfied herself that all guests had had their fill, then it was F.T.I. FAMILY TUCK IN, or in Gil's family F.U.A.I.K. FILL UP AFTER IN KITCHEN.

The piece de resistance for lunch that day, of which I was justly proud, was a lemon meringue pie. Unfortunately, as I was taking it from the oven, the door swung back onto my hand. It was hot, and as I automatically jerked my hand away I lost my grip on the pie, which fell face down onto the stone floor. I could have howled with fury when I saw my pie, meringue peaks browned to perfection, flattened beyond recognition. Quickly and furtively I scraped it off the flagstones, sprinkled the top with desiccated coconut, and remembering the old saying "What the eye doesn't see the heart can't grieve over" bore it triumphantly to the table, where it was acclaimed a culinary masterpiece.

"Lovely," said Dee, holding out her plate for a second helping. "What's it called?"

"Coconut Surprise," I said.

We picnicked in the New Forest on the Sunday, choosing to show our American guest a beautiful part of the forest near Lyndhurst known as the Ornamental Drive, a long pathway between high banks of rhododendrons, at that time tightly budded, but a week or two later bursting into breathtaking mauves and pinks. The air was cool as we sat cushioned on patches of purple heather, to eat our lunch. Moments of brilliant sunshine broke through the cloud, lighting up the tops of the birch trees and turning the gorse to gold. In the distance a group of ponies, thin after the hard and hungry winter, grazed with unceasing concentration on the fresh spring growth.

It was a merry lunch, washed down with a glass of Granny Watts' potato wine, and drifted on into the late afternoon, until it became apparent that word had reached the local wood ant colony that there was a large fruit cake in the forest, and it was not long before they arrived for their share. They marched in unseemly haste across the check cloth, three times the size of our Homestead ants, pausing on their way to take in a grain of sugar here and a crumb there, until Gil, his last encounter still a painful memory, leapt to his feet suggesting that either we leave or I ask them to leave. I was sure that on such short acquaintance they would not be too receptive, and I was not prepared to put it to the test against a background of giggling scepticism. So we shook ants and crumbs from the cloth and left them to their feast.

We could not let Beth go back to London without introducing her to another aspect of our culture, the English pub, and felt there could be no quainter example than "The Haven" at Mudeford. As we walked along the raised wooden walkway, there being no possibility of taking the van across the mud flats at high tide, the gulls dipped and screamed round the square black painted inn which stood out starkly against the pink streaked evening sky, a mysterious old place which one could imagine caught up in the smuggling which, a hundred years before, took place along the Dorset coast.

Beth was wide eyed with delight at the sight and sound which met us as we entered, and must have wondered at the eccentricities of a race which takes pleasure in herding together like cattle in such uncomfortable circumstances. The small room with its low beamed ceiling stained dark brown with decades of rising smoke, was already full of holidaymakers, and here and there could be seen a regular customer, an old sea salt in blue jersey and peaked cap spinning a tall yarn to an eager listener.

The high backed wooden seats against the wall were filled, and as we pushed our way through the noisy crowd the strains of "Nellie Dean" came from an old upright piano, thumped out with more enthusiasm than accuracy by an old hag with greasy hair and a cardigan to match, and a shrivelled face as brown as the ceiling. She was kept supplied by regulars and holidaymakers alike with half pints of beer, which stood in a row along the top, spilling their contents as the piano shook and shuddered under the onslaught from her filthy claws. At frequent intervals she vamped with her left hand while emptying a glass with her right like someone who has entered a piano playing marathon and dare not stop for fear of disqualification. Having slaked her thirst, she gave the patrons a solo performance of "Stop your tickling, Jock" with cackles of laughter and screeching high notes. Everyone joined in, applauded her loudly, and maintained her supply of beer.

The sing-song was gathering momentum as we left, stunned by sound and scarcely able to breath, and before walking back along the path to the van we sat for a moment on the quay, filling our lungs with the fresh salt air and looking out over the dark water.

We all agreed that it had been a good day, and after a last cup of coffee, yawned our way to bed. As I blew out the candle I lay listening to the quiet murmur of voices from the bedroom, and the rustling of the insomnious sparrows overhead. Many holes had appeared in the thatch, and we knew that wiring the whole roof was the most effective deterrent, but this was a costly process and it was to be the following spring before we felt able to justify the outlay. Even then, a small proportion of undersized birds wriggled their way through the mesh and we were never entirely free of nocturnal twitterings.

The sound of screams dragged us back to full consciousness, and we leapt up, flinging open the bedroom door to see the girls huddled together on the bed, their heads covered in bedclothes. The cause of their terror, three kamikaze maybugs attracted by the light from the lamp on the dressing table were dive bombing them, their hard brown wing cases hitting the walls with a loud crack. Gil ran downstairs to fetch a tennis racket as a weapon, and met Maurice on his way up fiercely brandishing a rolled news paper. Accompanied by stifled squeals from the bed the two intrepid, pyjama clad knights went into the offensive, laying about them with cries of "Tally-ho!" "Gottcha!" and "One down, two to go!" until the last stunned corpse was thrown through the window, and two white faces re-emerged. Maurice said "I'll fetch the first aid kit", and returned with a hip flask of brandy insisting that the girls take a "purely medicinal" sip.

Before many moments we were all sitting on the bed passing round the flask, all thoughts of sleep abandoned, and laughing heartily at what Maurice described as an original ending to a splendid day.

When finally lights were extinguished, windows firmly closed and peace descended on the Homestead I noticed that the sparrows had been stunned into total silence by the commotion below and had joined us in slumber.

Chapter 22

Rain spattered against the glass and ran in rivulets from the eaves as, dry and warm, we moved along the rows of plants, picking for the following morning's market. We were now up to full quantity and the quality of the fruit was well up to expectations, the trusses full and firm and a promising start to the season.

It was late in the afternoon when we carried the boxes up to the garage to be weighed and packed, having earlier taken our guests to catch the London train. Before they left, waving enthusiastically from the carriage window, growing smaller until one small hand was all that was visible, all had agreed that it had been a good weekend, a few days of laughter and friendship, a happy chance, and quite simply, quaint.

As we worked we heard the familiar pop-pop of Miss Foster's bicycle as it neared the cottage, and the "Cooee!" as the footsteps approached the garage. We were delighted to see her, our first "regular" of the year, and by far our favourite, knowing that we could always rely on her for some gossip or some fey observation or other, at the same time knowing that we would never grow fat on the profits from her purchases.

"Hello, dears," she said breathlessly, settling herself on a box. "If you've any chats I'll have a pound, but if not I'll just stay and have a chat!" and laughed so heartily at her joke that her pince nez fell off her dripping nose, and she sat wobbling with mirth, looking for all the world in her bright yellow mackintosh and matching souwester with the elastic under the chin, like an animated custard.

She mentioned what to us could be exciting news, that she had seen a man working on the transformer opposite Miss Lovejoy's house. Could it possibly mean that at last we were going to get our electricity supply? On enquiry it turned out to be the case, and at agonisingly infrequent intervals a new pole sprang up along the lane. At least we knew the work was in progress, however slowly, but it was to be another three frustrating months before we were able to consign the oil lamps to the store room.

Long stemmed sweet peas stood in bright profusion in buckets, waiting to be bunched and boxed, beautiful blooms for which we knew we would be paid one and sixpence, an excellent price at that time. Miss Foster left to make her way home, her tomatoes in the deep basket on the front of her bicycle and a bunch of sweet peas strapped to the back, with the compliments of the house, much to her delight.

The rain had eased off by then, and as we worked we were treated to an exuberant song from the blackbird from the topmost branch of Pok-Pok's tree, joyous fluting notes, ending with what sounded to us like frivolous variations on some other bird's repertoire.

After a short tea we continued well into the evening, determined to have everything boxed and stacked ready for the morning when Jim, our wholesaler's lorry driver, would be collecting. He was a little man with a wrinkled walnut face, whose one passion was gardening, and he knew by heart the botanical name of every flower and shrub, only he pronounced it "batonical."

Maud, who was sitting on the box vacated by Miss Foster, sat with round watchful eyes as a moth flew into the white, hissing light of the Tilley lamp, dealing it a swift blow as it fluttered near, where it fell to the ground, its fragile wings folded and frayed.

The job done, we stretched our aching backs and lit cigarettes, standing in the dark listening for a moment to the soft splash of the rats in the stream bank. The scent of honeysuckle and wet grass was strong after the rain, and Tack was already on his tour of inspection, his keen nose alert for any unusual visitor to his territory after the heavy showers.

Tired and grubby, we nodded over a late supper, and before going to bed Gil went down to tuck up the plants, returning a moment later smiling broadly and saying "All's well. The nightingale's back. Come and listen." We stood on the doorstep, spellbound, all tiredness forgotten, as the sweet song of the nightingale, so long silent, soared into the still night air, the pure haunting notes filling the garden with their magic.

Joan Simcock was born in Hampshire and educated in Upper Norwood and St. Albans. She trained and worked as a secretary in London until the outbreak of war, when she moved to Wiltshire with her family and worked on a farm before joining the A.T.S. After the war she married and acquired a smallholding in Dorset, and many years later, a keen amateur painter, she and her husband opened an art gallery in Bournemouth, where they remained until their retirement. They have a daughter and two grandchildren.